THE BIGGEST LOSER

dessert

COOKBOOK

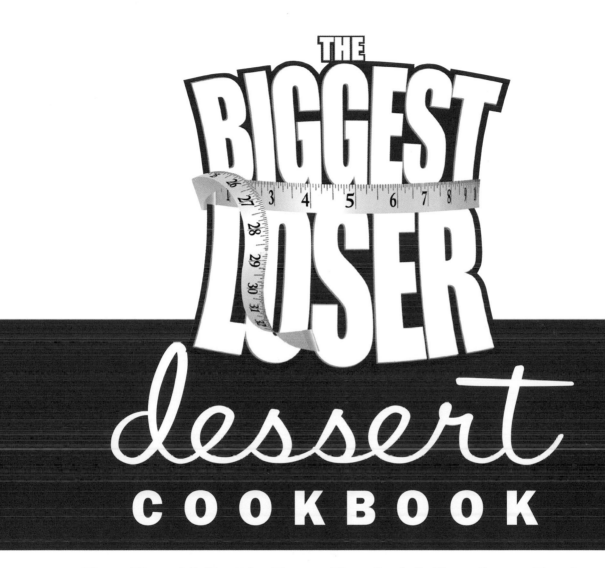

THE BIGGEST LOSER

dessert

COOKBOOK

**More Than 80 Healthy Treats That Satisfy Your Sweet Tooth
Without Breaking Your Calorie Budget**

Chef Devin Alexander and *The Biggest Loser* Experts and Cast

with Melissa Roberson

NBC

Rodale books may be purchased for business or promotional use or for special sales. For information, please write to:
Special Markets Department, Rodale, Inc., 733 Third Avenue, New York, NY 10017.

Printed in the United States of America
Rodale Inc. makes every effort to use acid-free ♾, recycled paper ♻.

Book design by Christina Gaugler
Illustration on page 21 by Judy Newhouse
Food photographs by Mitch Mandel and Tom McDonald/Rodale Images
Food styling by Diane Vezza and prop styling by Pamela Simpson
All other photos by NBC Universal Photo

Library of Congress Cataloging-in-Publication Data

Alexander, Devin.
    The biggest loser dessert cookbook : more than 80 healthy treats that satisfy your sweet tooth without breaking your calorie budget / Devin Alexander, Melissa Roberson.
        p.   cm.
    Includes index.
    ISBN 978–1–60961–129–3 pbk
    1. Desserts.   2. Reducing diets—Recipes.   3. Biggest loser (Television program)   I. Roberson, Melissa.   II. Title.
TX773.A345 2010
641.8'6—dc22   2010040302

Distributed to the trade by Macmillan
2   4   6   8   10   9   7   5   3   1   paperback

We inspire and enable people to improve their lives and the world around them.

Production Development & Direction: Chad Bennett, Dave Broome, Joni Camacho, Steve Coulter, Mark Koops, Todd Nelson, Kim Niemi, J. D. Roth, Neysa Siefert, and Ben Silverman

NBCU, Reveille, 25/7 Productions, and 3Ball Productions would like to thank the many people who gave their time and energy to this project: Stephen Andrade, Carole Angelo, Dana Arnett, Sebastian Attie, Nancy N. Bailey, *The Biggest Loser* contestants, Dave Bjerke, Maria Bohe, Jill Bowles, Jen Busch, Jill Carmen, Scot Chastain, Ben Cohen, Jason Cooper, Marie Crousillat, Dan Curran, Dr. Michael Dansinger, Camilla Dhanak, Devin Franchino, Kat Elmore, John Farrell, Cheryl Forberg, Jeff Friedman, Jeff Gaspin, Christina Gaugler, Marc Graboff, Jenny Groom, Bob Harper, Chris Harris, Robyn Hennessey, Shelli Hill, Dr. Robert Huizenga, Jill Jarosz, Helen Jorda, Adam Kaloustian, Edwin Karapetian, Alex Katz, Allison Kaz, Loretta Kraft, Laura Kuhn, Beth Lamb, Todd Lubin, Roni Lubliner, Alan Lundgren, Carole MacDonal, Rebecca Marks, Jillian Michaels, Gregg Michaelson, John Miller, Sarah Napier, Yelena Nesbit, Julie Nugent, Trae Patton, Ellie Prezant, Ed Prince, Scott Radloff, Lee Rierson Rierson, Karen Rinaldi, Melissa Roberson, Beth Roberts, Maria Rodale, Jessica Roth, Drew Rowley, Leslie Schwartz, Robin Shallow, Carrie Simons, Lee Straus, Kella Tardiff, Paul Telegdy, Deborah Thomas, Julie True, Josie Ventura, Emily Weber, Liza Whitcraft, Julie Will, Audrey Wood, Yong Yam, Jeff Zucker

Contents

Introduction

"I've lost more than 55 pounds, and 16 years later, I still eat chocolate *every* day."

That's the first thing I say at pretty much every cooking demonstration, lecture, and keynote speech I give around the country. And it's true. You too can eat chocolate (or another dessert) daily, if you want to . . . as long as you do it the right way.

I've been working with *The Biggest Loser* for more than four years now in a variety of capacities, but one of my favorite roles has been meeting the contestants and showing them how they can indulge in healthy ways—giving them the freedom to eat the foods they love and satisfy their cravings without sacrificing their weight loss goals.

For me, the key to maintaining a substantial weight loss has been regularly allowing myself healthy indulgences so that I never feel deprived. Many times, people who are trying to lose or maintain a weight loss think they can't ever eat sweets again. And while it's true that the unhealthiest foods should probably stay off-limits the vast majority of the time, you can satisfy your sweet cravings in a multitude of ways without breaking your calorie budget.

I should know. For years I've been creating recipes for friends, family, clients, and cookbooks (not to mention for me!) that are big on flavor and low in calories. When you start flipping through the pages of this book and see the photographs of Strawberry Daiquiri Cream Pie (page 55), Blueberry Cream Cheese "Strudel" (page 143), and Chocolate Hazelnut Ricotta Calzones (page 148), you're likely to think, *There's no way I can eat that and be healthy!* But once you take a look at the nutritional data, you'll realize that you can have your cake and lose weight, too.

Most dessert cookbooks are organized by ingredient (such as "chocolate") or type of item (such as "cakes"), but we wanted to create a format that makes sense for the way you and your family live. That's why you'll find chapters on snacks, drinks, frozen treats, holiday baking, and even a whole chapter devoted to on-the-go treats that are easy to whip up for bake sales, PTA meetings, and kids' classroom parties. The only exception to this rule is Chapter 3, "A Passion for Fruit." We wanted to start off the cookbook with an array of fruit-based treats because fruit is such an important part of *The Biggest Loser* plan, and we recommend it as the first choice any time a sweet craving strikes. But with delicious recipes like Naked Apple Tart (page 44), Meringue-Topped Pink Grapefruit (page 51), and Peach Blackberry Betty (page 59) fruit practically feels like an indulgence!

These days there are an abundance of "healthy" treats and snacks available at grocery stores, bakeries, and specialty food markets. But while they may be convenient, many of these lower-fat, lower-calorie foods rely on artificial ingredients to make them taste good. All of the recipes in this book are made with only natural ingredients, allowing you to create all-natural goodies that you'll be proud to share with friends and family and happy to feed to your kids.

I believe that in order to live a healthy life, you have to befriend food—it's not the enemy!—and allow yourself to enjoy the things you love, in moderation. As long as you cook and bake at home, you have control over every calorie that goes onto your plate (and into your mouth). You can create the flavors you love and still lose weight—I'm living proof of that.

It's truly an honor to be a part of *The Biggest Loser* community, and I am looking forward to hearing from each and every one of you—about your weight-loss successes to the kinds of recipes you want to see in the next book!

Dessert anyone?

Chef Devin Alexander

Notes to the Chef, from the Chef

While the recipes in this book are definitely easy enough for even novice cooks to whip up, it never hurts to have a few extra tips up your sleeve as well as an understanding of the "why" behind the instructions. Also, because this book incorporates ingredients that you may not be familiar with—and because lower-fat baked goods do have some simple yet important "rules" for success—I've compiled a few basic guidelines that I hope will assist you in creating the perfect healthy and decadent treats. I'd recommend perusing them before you start making any of these recipes.

Testing Doneness of Baked Goods

You'll notice that when it's time to test the doneness of baked goods with a toothpick, I instruct "a few crumbs are okay." You probably already know that when making baked goods made with butter and/or oil, you want a toothpick to come out clean and dry. But very low-fat and fat-free baked goods will be slightly sticky and crumby in the center when fully cooked. In a few recipes (such as the Strawberry-Filled Brownie Bites, page 156), I do use a small amount of oil in the batter, so the toothpick should come out cleaner. But in all other recipes, make sure you remove the baked goods from the oven at that stage. If you cook them until the toothpick is completely dry, they will overcook.

Processing Flours

Many of the recipes in this book call for whole grain oat flour, whole wheat pastry flour, or a combination of the two. Unlike the enriched white all-purpose flour that most Americans are used to baking with, oat flour and wheat flour can sometimes have a gritty texture (depending on the brand you use), which is why I often instruct you to process the flours in a food processor before using them. Though it takes a little extra time, processing the flours is important because it produces a finer texture, which will help yield a better finished product.

Fresh-Squeezed Juice

I strongly advise against using bottled lemon or lime juice (which contain citric acid and often other preservatives) in any of these recipes. I know it can be tempting to take a shortcut and use the bottled stuff, but the tiny amount of time you might save just plain isn't worth it. I swear! Freshly squeezed lemon and lime juice imparts a unique, bright flavor that can't be matched by the bottled stuff. So when life gives you lemons, please take my advice and make *fresh-squeezed* lemonade!

Yogurt Cheese

One of my favorite recipes in the book, Mini Key Lime Cheesecake Pies (page 139), calls for fat-free Yogurt Cheese (page 218). Yogurt cheese is plain yogurt that has been strained (in this case, through a clean dish towel) of any excess liquid, leaving you with a thick, creamy cheese, much like cream cheese. I actually prefer it to fat-free cream cheese because it's all-natural and doesn't have an aftertaste. Making yogurt cheese might seem like a bit of trouble to go through at first, but the end result is definitely worth it. No one who has tasted my cheesecake pies has ever suspected they're made with yogurt—everyone thinks it's full-fat cream cheese. Plus making yogurt cheese is a great project to do with your kids!

Baking Pans

Did you know that the color of your baking pans can affect the baking time and doneness of your baked goods? Recipes baked in dark metal pans tend to cook a lot quicker than when they're baked in lighter pans. Think about it: When you stand on white pavement in the summer, your feet get hot. But when you stand on a surface of black pavement, the heat is unbearable. The darker color concentrates the heat from the sun the way darker pans concentrate heat in the oven. In general, I prefer pans with a coating that is light or medium gray to those that are dark gray or black. In darker pans, the edges cook more quickly and thus can get tough as the inside cooks through. If you only have darker pans, it's best to lower the oven temperature 25 degrees to accommodate them.

Fun-Shaped Dishes and Minis

You may have heard me say this before, but I just can't emphasize it enough (especially when it comes to eating healthy): We eat with our eyes first. If something looks yummy and appetizing, even if it's just a simple fruit salad served in a martini glass, it's more of a "treat" because it looks special. So when I'm making desserts, I like to keep things interesting by using fun-shaped pans or dishes. I love making cupcakes in cute silicone cupcake molds (Tovolo has a lot of cool holiday themed shapes and Fred & Friends also offers an adorable selection of fun molds) or making custards in pretty, fluted individual glass dishes. Making things "mini" also ensures better portion control—you're probably less likely to eat two "mini" pies than you are to nibble at an entire pie or go back for just "one more little sliver." I urge you to get creative in your kitchen with mini muffin tins, tart and cake pans, silicone baking molds, festive bakeware, and popsicle molds to create healthy dessert-making fun for you and your family.

Lining with Parchment Paper

By lining your dish with parchment paper, you ensure that ingredients won't stick to the dish—plus cleanup will be easier. When lining to make something delicate like a cake, you want to actually trace the pan on the parchment and make sure it fits snugly with no wrinkles. When baking something less precise, like Chocolate-Glazed Soft Pretzel Bites (page 82), you just want to cut a piece of parchment paper slightly narrower than the dish and set it inside (if it goes up the sides a bit on two ends, that's okay). You don't, however, want to cut such a large piece of parchment that it goes above the edges of the dish or else it could potentially burn in the oven. And please don't use waxed paper in place of parchment paper—I know it's less expensive, and though it is great for some uses, it doesn't always work as a substitute for parchment paper.

Foil or Silicone Cupcake Liners

Many of the recipes in this book call for foil or silicone cupcake liners to line muffin pans. That's because low-fat muffins and cupcakes have so little fat that much of the muffin will stick to paper liners. Be careful when separating a stack of foil cups, as there are typically paper liners in between each cup that should be discarded. If you can't find foil or silicone cups, a good nonstick pan lightly coated with cooking spray will allow you to skip the liners altogether.

Oven Temperature

Did you know that most home ovens are purposely calibrated to be 25 degrees *lower* than the actual temperature dial? I've learned this from multiple oven repair people and appliance company representatives. They do it because over time, ovens tend to become hotter. This may not matter much when you're cooking your dinner. But baked goods are much more sensitive to fluctuations in temperature. So if you feel like your oven runs cold or hot, I'd suggest using an oven thermometer on one of your oven racks to see if it matches your temperature dial.

Also, though many people make it a habit of lining the bottom of their oven with aluminum foil, this actually interferes with your oven temperature. The reflection of the foil creates a concentration of heat on the bottom of the oven, preventing the heat from surrounding your food evenly. If you're really worried about spillage, it's best to use a silicone oven liner on the bottom of your oven.

Ice Cream Maker

There are many commercial ice cream makers available these days at varying prices. If you're a huge ice cream lover and want your healthy ice creams and yogurts quickly, I'd definitely invest in a compressor model. If you're an occasional ice cream eater or if you have children who will enjoy cranking the ice cream themselves, you can get an ice and rock salt machine. Lastly, there are also the popular freezer bowl models, which are metal bowls that contain a special liquid freezing solution. The bowl needs to be frozen before you make the ice cream, so plan accordingly.

Whatever model you choose, just make sure you read the manufacturer's instructions carefully, and you'll be on your way to making delicious low-fat ice creams and sorbets like none available on the market today!

Egg Whites vs. Egg Substitute vs. Liquid Egg Whites

You'll note that some recipes call for egg whites, while others call for egg substitute. If you're familiar with egg substitute and liquid egg whites, you'll notice that they are not as thick as egg whites that you extract from a whole egg. Thus they are not necessarily swappable in recipes. You sometimes need the "body" of the actual white to give body to your baked goods. If there is too much liquid, baked goods can get tough or overcook on the outside before the inside is cooked through. So please follow the exact instructions for eggs whenever possible.

Sweet Shopping

When I was asked to create an all-natural dessert book that didn't contain *any* processed sugars or flours or other processed ingredients, I knew that the task would require more than a little ingenuity. I also knew that making desserts that taste great would require some unique ingredients that may be a bit challenging to find but that are most certainly worth the effort to hunt down.

To make things a little easier for you, I've created this shopping guide. I hope it helps you discover how to find new or lesser-known ingredients that will make you healthier and happier.

100% Fruit Spreads and Preserves

Who knew these could be used for so much more than just PB&J or your morning toast? Be sure to double-check labels and buy spreads or preserves that say "100% fruit." You don't want to buy fruit spreads that are filled with added sugars or sweeteners (like high-fructose corn syrup). Also, carefully pour out any excess liquid floating around at the top of the jar, which would add unwanted moisture to your baked goods.

Agave Nectar

Also sometimes referred to as "agave syrup," this sweetener is produced from the Mexican agave plant. To put it simply, juice is extracted from this plant, then concentrated into a syrupy liquid about the thickness of honey. The variation in colors (from light to dark) depends on the degree the juice is processed. You'll find agave sold in clear, light, blue, amber, dark, and raw varieties. You can also find flavored agaves, such as amaretto, Irish cream, and vanilla.

Clear and light agaves have a pretty mild, neutral flavor and are great for delicate baked goods (please note, "light" refers only to the color, not the calories). Light agave tends to be less expensive than clear, though most brands are pretty similar in flavor, so I usually opt for light. Blue and amber agaves have a more discernable caramel flavor, so they're fine for desserts where other strong flavors are present (such as banana or mocha). Dark agave nectar has a much stronger caramel flavor, so I don't recommend using it for the recipes in this book.

Raw agave comes in different varieties. For a food to be truly considered "raw," it shouldn't be heated above 118°F, but regulations for raw food aren't very strict. Make sure to do some research before buying raw agave, which can be expensive. You want to be sure you're getting a quality product.

Unlike honey (which is probably the most popular natural sugar alternative and has a strong, distinct flavor), I've found agave to have a more subtle flavor, much like granulated sugar. Look for it in grocery stores, natural food stores, and online (it can even be purchased in bulk from many online retailers, if you want to save money). Please note that throughout this book, I specify which type of agave to use when it matters. If no color is specified, then clear, light, amber, or blue agave would be fine.

Almond Milk

Almond milk is made from ground almonds that are soaked and blended with water and then drained. Unsweetened almond milk has only about 40 calories per cup! Unlike fat-free dairy milk (which has about 90 calories per cup), almond milk is cholesterol free and lactose free. Many commercial almond milks are available in plain and (sweetened and unsweetened) vanilla and chocolate flavors. I've found that not all almond milks are created equal—some brands definitely taste better than others, so if you try one and don't like it, try another brand. Also, note that although almond milk is low in calories, it does contain some fat (about 3 grams per cup).

Cacao Nibs

All chocolate is made from the cacao (cocoa) bean. Cacao beans in their natural, unprocessed state are rich in nutrients and beneficial to health. Cacao nibs are as healthy as "chocolate" gets because they have no added sugars and are raw and unprocessed. They can be found at most natural food stores.

Cocoa Powder

When buying cocoa powder, make sure you choose one that contains "cocoa" as the single ingredient. Not all cocoa powders taste the same, so if you try one and don't love the results it produces in your baked goods, try a different one. Cost isn't necessarily a factor—there are many inexpensive cocoas that taste very good.

Coconut (Palm) Sugar

You'll find that a lot of recipes in this book call for coconut sugar. Though it doesn't taste like white granulated sugar, it works very well to make desserts taste like those made from sugar. You may also see it labeled as "palm sugar" or "coconut palm sugar"; that's because it's harvested from the sap of coconut palms. It's completely natural and has a very low glycemic index (it won't cause your blood sugar to spike). Admittedly, it can be a bit expensive and challenging to find, but it is gaining popularity and becoming more common. I recommend looking for it in the bulk bins at your local natural or health food store or even in the natural food aisle of major grocery chains. It's also available for purchase online.

Please note that because coconut (palm) sugar is so new to the market, there are discrepancies in exactly how many calories it contains. I based all of the calorie counts in this book on the estimation of 15 calories per teaspoon.

Also note that while *The Biggest Loser* food plan suggests you consume sugar only in very small quantities, if you cannot locate coconut (palm) sugar, you can substitute an equal amount of unpacked brown sugar for similar results.

Dark Chocolate

It's no secret that I *love* chocolate, and I simply couldn't write an entire dessert book without including some chocolate. Like red wine, small amounts of dark chocolate have been linked to health benefits (like improving cardiovascular health) because they contain flavanoids, which are powerful antioxidants. In order to get these benefits, you must consume chocolate that is 70 percent or more pure cocoa, so make sure to check the label on your chocolate chunks or chocolate bar before you buy.

Dried Fruit

You would think something as seemingly healthy as dried fruit wouldn't require further explanation, but did you know that many commercial dried fruits contain added sugars, preservatives, and oils? Read labels carefully to make sure your dried fruit is 100 percent fruit, with no added sugars or oils, and whenever possible, choose "unsulfured" fruit. Sulfur dioxide is a preservative used to extend the shelf life of dried fruit. Studies have suggested that, over time, consuming large amounts of sulfites and other preservatives can be harmful to your health.

Dry-Roasted Nuts

We all know that nuts are good for us but that they need to be eaten in moderation because they are high in fat and calories. I recommend that you buy and use dry-roasted nuts. "Dry roasted" means the nuts have been roasted without any added oils or fats. If you can afford to have a little extra salt in your diet, I recommend you look for dry-roasted and lightly salted nuts, since they taste even better in some recipes where the sweet-salty balance really makes a difference.

Edible Glitter

I *love* using edible glitter to add festive color and sparkle to baked goods, without any of the calories that traditional colored sprinkles or colored sugars contain. Most edible glitter is a mixture of gum arabic (the hardened sap of the Acacia senegal tree) and water. Always check the ingredient list and nutrition label of a product to make sure it doesn't contain sugar. A popular (and inexpensive) product I like to use is called Wilton's cake sparkles. You can find them at many craft stores in the cake decorating aisle. You can also look for edible glitter in cake-decorating stores, in specialty food stores, or at online retailers.

Fat-Free Evaporated Milk

I decided to include a brief note on this ingredient because I want to be sure no one mistakes evaporated milk for sweetened condensed milk, which is very different. Evaporated milk is fresh milk with about 60 percent of the water removed, but it has no sugar added to it. Both are canned, so they will likely be in the same aisle of your grocery store; be sure not to confuse the two.

Fat-Free, Fruit Juice–Sweetened Yogurt

Obviously yogurt is great just for eating on its own, but I often use it in baked goods, too. While there are plenty of naturally sweetened plain yogurts available at the supermarket, there was only one brand of fruit-juice sweetened, flavored, fat-free yogurt I could find across most of the country: Cascade Fresh. Luckily, it's sold in 49 out of 50 states (sorry, Delaware), and comes in lots of delicious flavors like Green Apple Pie, Cherry Vanilla, and Apricot Mango (and, of course, vanilla is available as well). If you don't see Cascade Fresh at your local grocery store, ask your dairy department if they can get it for you, since it's likely distributed in your state already. Or check your local natural food store.

If you really can't find it, you can substitute any brand of fat-free yogurt for equally delicious results. Just bear in mind that *The Biggest Loser* food plan recommends using products made with unprocessed sugars.

Finely Shredded Reduced-Fat Unsweetened Coconut

This is a great natural alternative to the sweetened flaked coconut most of us are used to (which often contains corn syrup) and still adds that crave-able coconut flavor to recipes. Any brand you can find is fine, though Let's Do . . . Organic is a great one that seems to be the most popular at my local natural food stores.

Gelatin

Some brands of gelatin contain more calories than others. A very popular brand, Knox, is 25 calories per 0.25-ounce packet, though I've seen others that are up to 30 calories for the same amount of gelatin. In recipes where gelatin isn't a main ingredient, that small variable won't make much of a difference. But if you're making something like the Sparkling Black Cherry Squares (page 87), and you're really watching your caloric intake, you might want to choose a brand that's lower in calories.

Graham Crackers

There are a few varieties of all-natural whole wheat graham crackers to choose from out there. When selecting a brand, you definitely want to watch out for no-no ingredients like hydrogenated oils and sugars (sometimes listed as "corn syrup" or "cane juice"). Instead, look for ingredients like whole wheat flour (not enriched whole wheat flour) and natural (nonsugar) sweeteners such as honey and molasses. I particularly like New Morning Organic Honey Grahams, which I purchase at a local natural food store.

Hazelnut Butter

Throughout the development phase of this book, I experimented with recipes that used different nut butters. They impart great flavor in a lot of dishes, and though they are high in fat, they also contain a high concentration of nutrients. All-natural nut butters are pretty easy to find these days. I prefer hazelnut butter made from nuts that are first dry-roasted (meaning, they are roasted with no added oil or fats). It has a stronger, more decadent flavor than hazelnut butter made from raw nuts. If you can't find that, just make sure the hazelnut butter you use (or any nut butter for that matter) doesn't contain added oils, sugars, or too much sodium.

Instant Espresso Powder

Coffee and espresso are great flavors on their own, but I especially love using espresso to enhance the richness of chocolate desserts. Spiking chocolate baked goods and custards with a little instant espresso powder is a great way to add depth of flavor without adding many calories. Just be sure to store any unused espresso in your freezer—it will last much longer and stay fresher that way.

Omega-3 Eggs

These eggs have three to six times the amount of omega-3 found in regular eggs (this is because they come from chickens that eat diets rich in omega-3). You actually have to eat the yolks in these eggs to get the omega-3 benefits. Needless to say, they tend to be substantially more expensive than most traditional eggs, which is why I specifically list them only in recipes that use the entire egg (white and yolk).

Pomegranate Molasses

This may sound like an exotic ingredient, but it's actually just unsweetened pomegranate juice that has been reduced down to a thick, dark syrup. It's an ingredient popular in Middle Eastern cooking for both sweet and savory dishes. It has a very concentrated pomegranate flavor and can be purchased at many specialty foods stores, natural food stores, and many liquor retailers.

Short-Grain Brown Rice Bowls

If you think you don't like brown rice, maybe it's because you haven't tried short-grain brown rice. It has a great texture and nutty flavor that I love. It does take a little extra time to cook on the stove, but there are lots of delicious ready-made, all-natural short-grain brown rices out there, such as fully cooked microwaveable brown rice bowls and frozen brown rice. One of my favorite brands is GoGo Rice bowls because they have no additives whatsoever, they're shelf-stable, and they're ready in 1½ minutes!

Stevia

This all-natural sugar substitute has zero calories and is 30 times sweeter than sugar. Stevia doesn't adversely affect blood glucose levels, so it's great for diabetics and anyone watching their sugar intake. It comes in different forms, such as powder, tablets, and liquid drops as well as different flavors, from Irish Creme to English Toffee. A couple of the more popular brands are Truvia and SweetLeaf. While stevia is great for many applications, I prefer not to bake with it. I use agave or coconut sugar to achieve more decadent results.

Stevia-Sweetened Soda

Diet, zero-calorie soda has been around for years, but it's typically made with aspartame, sucralose, or other chemical-based sweeteners. Now there are natural alternatives available made with stevia (see above). Check out the natural food aisle of your grocery store and health food stores to find your favorite traditional soda flavor made with stevia.

Sugar Cones

Though I don't recommend using these often, I like to keep them in my pantry when I'm in the mood for something sweet and crunchy, like my Conenolis (page 76). Look for cones that are made with wheat flour, such as Let's Do . . . Organic's Organic Sugar Cones, which I find at my local health food store.

Whole Grain Naturally Sweetened Cereals

Truth be told, finding whole grain cereals sweetened with anything but processed sugar is a bit of a challenge. Though many claim to be whole grain, one quick glance at the nutritional panel reveals a lot more sugar than whole grains. Luckily, I found a couple of brands that deliver on both nutrition and taste. Kashi 7 Whole Grain Nuggets are great crushed and made into a pie crust, and Barbara's Bakery has a number of whole grain, fruit juice–sweetened cereals (I especially love the Cinnamon Crunch and Vanilla Almond varieties). I also use brown rice cereal for my Crispy Peanut Butter Squares (page 137).

Whole Grain Oat Flour

All flours have different levels of starch and gluten, so they bake differently and will lend different textures to finished dishes. I love using whole grain oat flour because it can create desserts that have a flavor and texture very similar to those traditionally made with all-purpose flour. Oat flour is simply made from finely ground oats. In fact, you can even grind old-fashioned oats in your food processor and make your own oat flour. It's also available in many major grocery stores (just check the natural food aisle), your local health food store, and online.

Whole Wheat Pastry Flour

This is different from white flours because not all of the bran and germ portions of the wheat kernel are removed during milling. This flour is produced from soft wheat, and it has a fine texture and high starch content. It's more nutritious than white flour, but much denser. When I use whole wheat pastry flour, I typically like to combine it with oat flour and process it in the food processor to create a finer texture. Whole wheat pastry flour is available in most major grocery stores, health food stores, and online.

Whole Wheat Pizza Dough

I love using whole wheat pizza dough to make more than just pizza—it's great for homemade pretzels and breads and can be a healthier (and easier) alternative to phyllo dough. It's also a great "shortcut" ingredient, since quality whole wheat doughs can be purchased at many local grocery stores and/or pizzerias. Just make sure you buy dough that's free of "enriched" (processed) flour and low in fat—some pizza doughs are made with lots of oil, which you definitely want to avoid. Your dough should have no more than 3 grams of fat per 2-ounce serving.

How Sweet It Is

Each season on *The Biggest Loser*, we watch the contestants sweat their way to a sleeker body and a brand-new lease on life. Under the expert guidance of a team of medical and nutritional experts, not to mention the watchful eyes of trainers Bob Harper and Jillian Michaels, the contestants say goodbye to the unhealthy habits of their past—overeating, not exercising, taking the easy way out—and create a road map for their future that includes nourishing their bodies with wholesome foods and becoming more physically fit than they ever imagined possible.

But the dramatic, transformative changes we see unfold on our television screens are only a part of the story. In order for the contestants to continue their weight-loss journeys at home, they must learn how to develop healthy, sustainable habits they can adopt for the long haul. And that includes cultivating one key concept: balance.

After leaving *The Biggest Loser* Ranch, cast members learn how to enjoy the things they love—**in moderation**. Some contestants, like Season 5's Bernie Salazar, choose to enjoy favorite foods in smaller portions; others, like Season 8 Winner Danny Cahill, plan for limited splurges; still others, such as Season 7's Tara Costa, limit access to treats such as ice cream to special occasions. Maintaining a healthy lifestyle isn't about deprivation, just making smarter choices.

Another strategy the *Biggest Losers* employ when it comes to finding balance is learning how to transform their favorite "sinful" foods into guilt-free treats. Most of the contestants come to the Ranch with a serious sweet tooth, and desserts and sweet snacks are some of the hardest foods for them to part with. But they soon learn how to satisfy their cravings with healthier, lower-calorie versions of their favorite guilty pleasures. And when they choose a healthy indulgence over a high-calorie treat, they don't have to contend with the inevitable guilt that follows.

In this book, you'll find more than 80 recipes for desserts, snacks, sweet sips, and more that allow you to indulge in the flavors you love without undermining your weight-loss efforts. And even better, these delicious recipes were created with absolutely no fake stuff—you won't find any artificial food in these pages—just wholesome, natural ingredients that create the flavor you crave with a fraction of the calories you'd probably expect.

So how do you incorporate moderation and indulgence into a healthy lifestyle? We caught up with some *Biggest Loser* alumni to find out how sweet their lives are today and how they keep it that way.

Curtis Stone's Sweet Tips

Celebrity Chef Curtis Stone is no stranger to *The Biggest Loser* campus, making frequent guest appearances on the show and teaching the contestants how to cook healthy foods that are big on flavor and low in calories.

Here are some of Curtis's top tips for healthy eating without sacrifice.

- To avoid satisfying your sweet cravings with unhealthy foods, keep your kitchen stocked with fruit. When you don't keep snacks that are packed with fat and sugar in the house, then you eliminate the temptation to abandon your eating plan.

- A healthy dessert can be something as simple as fresh, seedless watermelon

pulp pureed in a blender and frozen in ice-pop molds. You get all of the nutrients and flavor of watermelon in a frozen dessert.

- Smoothies are always a hit, and you can get really creative with them. Try blending a banana with a small dollop of unsweetened all-natural creamy peanut butter, some fat-free milk or yogurt, and plenty of ice. You can even add a little protein powder for a balanced in-between-meal snack.

- Spices add a punch of flavor to almost any dish, including desserts. If you're baking with fruit or nuts, don't be afraid to experiment with cinnamon, allspice, cloves, and star anise. They create even more flavor without adding fat or sugar.

ASHLEY JOHNSTON Season 9 Runner-Up

Starting Weight: 374

Finale Weight: 191

Today's Weight: mid-180s

Ashley may not have won the competition, but she did set a new *Biggest Loser* record by losing 49 percent of her body weight by the Season 9 finale—more than any female contestant in history!

Ashley says the struggle with her weight took on momentum when she was a teenager, and she went on to gain more than 100 pounds. "I felt stuck in a body that did not allow me to live life, to be myself, to dress in the kind of clothes I like," she remembers.

When she lost her father to cancer, she hit rock bottom. "When he was sick, I ran from it," she admits. "I couldn't be around it. And I just let my weight get out of control."

A longtime fan of *The Biggest Loser*, Ashley knew the show could help her make the changes she needed to get healthy. "I figured if I could expose myself in front of America, there would be no turning back for me," she says. She convinced her mother, Sherry—who was also struggling with her weight after the loss of her husband—to try out for the show with her. They both made the cut.

Today, she says she's more confident than ever. "I've never lost weight before, only gained. To be able to get rid of old clothes because they're too large is an amazing feeling. I definitely feel more confident, secure, and sexy. My health is so much better, and my goals seem achievable and reachable."

Ashley says that she maintains balance in her life by working out with a trainer several days a week and training for her first half-triathlon. She's also learning to cook. She still enjoys her social life but puts more planning into her evenings, sometimes eating a healthy meal at home before going out, so that she's not tempted to overindulge. She says she still enjoys a glass or two of wine once a week, but not every other night.

"I sit here today having accomplished so much. That is what my dad wanted from me. That's all he really wanted was for me to be healthy and happy. And I've done it."

MICHAEL VENTRELLA *Season 9 Winner*

Starting Weight: 526

Finale Weight: 262

Today's Weight: 252

Michael has come a long way since his pre-*Biggest Loser* days, when he was happier asleep than awake. "It was so sad," he now admits. "I got to a point where my dreams were so much better than my reality. I didn't want to wake up in the morning because I was miserable."

Tipping the scales at 526 pounds—the show's heaviest contestant ever—Michael knew that at the young age of 31, his life was in the balance. He says at the time he thought, "I'm not married, I don't have kids. I'm not even close to it. The only thing I'm close to is probably dying."

But less than 5 months later, the former Chicago DJ broke another record when it was revealed that he had lost 264 pounds (beating Season 8 contestant Danny Cahill's record of 239 pounds) and took home the $250,000 grand prize!

Today, Michael is still working out every day to reach a healthier weight. "Figuring out the right amount of eating and exercising to keep losing and get to my ideal weight is an ongoing process," he says.

One thing is for sure: His eating habits have undergone a radical transformation, and he's learned how to embrace the concept of moderation. "I used to have an enormous sweet tooth. Now my cravings are less intense. I'll still enjoy a dessert every now and again, but I like to eat it with small spoon so I get more bites out of it and can savor it."

Michael says if he could go back and say something to his former overweight, sedentary, lost self—and anyone struggling with weight loss—it would be that there's hope. "Wake up," he says. "This is real. All it takes is really hard work. It's so worth it. Open yourself up to the process."

ERIK CHOPIN Season 3 Winner

Starting Weight: 407 pounds

Finale Weight: 193

Today's Weight: 245

As Bob Harper put it, Erik's transformation at his Season 3 finale was "absolutely jaw-dropping." But almost three years later, Bob showed up at Erik's house to confront a man who had regained more than 175 pounds.

"When I returned from the Ranch," says Erik, "I looked great on the outside, but internally I was still struggling. I wasn't sure that everything I learned was sticking. I maintained the weight loss for about a year and a half. There were things in my life that were keeping me accountable. But then I went back to my regular job, and I started putting the weight back on and soon was back up to 368 pounds."

Fearing disapproval from his former trainer, Erik was reassured by Bob. "I understand this," says Bob. "I understand how hard it is. It's my job. I see people every single day, and it's a struggle. I just wanted to come and see Erik and say, 'It's going to be okay.'"

Erik admits that the weight just crept back on as he allowed himself to go over his calorie budget more and more. Part of his struggle, he now realizes, is that he tried to maintain too strict of a lifestyle when he first returned home from the Ranch. But Bob encouraged him to find balance. "You've got to find a way that you can do this today to live the rest of your life," Bob told him. "You can't do the extreme. You've done the extreme."

Erik began working out at a boxing gym and slowly began losing again. He also went to *The Biggest Loser* Resort at Fitness Ridge for several weeks and says he "got into a groove" there. "Being at the resort rearranged my thinking. Eating healthy doesn't have to seem like deprivation," he admits.

Erik knows his story is different than some of the other contestants, and that's okay. It's *his* story. And now that he's finally found some balance, his story is headed toward a happy ending.

HOLLIE SELF Season 4

Starting Weight: 255

Finale Weight: 150

Today's Weight: 160

Hollie Self was one of those contestants who was always more interested in what went on behind the camera than in front. In fact, today she works for the production company that produces *The Biggest Loser*!

Three years after her time on the show, she's learned a thing or two about maintenance. "I think that all of the contestants expect that after the finale, life's going to be easy," she explains. "And it's not. It's been a few years of learning and trying to figure out how to make this work, how to make permanent changes."

"We know how to gain weight," she says. "We know how to lose weight, but maintaining? That's a whole different animal. That's a whole new set of skills you have to learn, and that's what I've been doing the last three years."

Her must-have tool? "You have to keep a food journal," she advises. "When things go a little awry, it's because I'm not writing it down." Plus she has found that there's no getting around working out several days a week. "I don't exercise every day, but I do exercise at least 5 days a week. That's nonnegotiable for me now."

She mixes things up by taking different classes at the gym, and she trains for triathlons and the occasional marathon. She was particularly thrilled to run in last year's New York City Marathon. "Crossing that finish line came right after my *Biggest Loser* finale in terms of excitement."

Hollie says long-term weight loss "is about finding balance. You will eat a cheeseburger again. There will be a day you can't make it to the gym. That's okay. You can eat out once in a while and have a cocktail every so often. But you have to get back on track the next day."

Does she offer advice when she's interviewing each season's new crop of *Biggest Loser* contestants? "I leave it up to them," she says. "It's their journey, and I'm very committed to each person having his or her own experience."

MATT HOOVER Season 2 Winner

Starting Weight: 339
Finale Weight: 182
Today's Weight: 245

SUZY PRESTON Season 2 Finalist

Starting Weight: 227
Finale Weight: 132
Today's Weight: 175

Matt's whole world changed after his time on *The Biggest Loser*. Not only was he the Season 2 winner, but he also met his future wife on the Ranch, fellow contestant Suzy Preston. Sparks began to fly when Matt, who arrived at the Ranch a messy mop of hair, invited Suzy, a hairdresser, to cut it all off. Matt and Suzy both remember it today as a special moment that bonded the two of them.

Matt is now a motivational speaker and life coach, and Suzy continues to work as a hairdresser. They live with their two sons, Rex and Jax, in Seattle.

"When we became parents, our number-one goal was to have them not struggle like we have with our weights," says Matt. "So we're really focused on eating healthy and being active as a family. It's not like 'Daddy's exercising.' We do things together as a family. My son Rex has done two 5-Ks."

Suzy, who admits she is still battling baby weight, is training for a triathlon to keep her focused. But the kind of workouts they used to put in on the Ranch? No way. These days, it's all about creating a sustainable lifestyle. "I don't have time to work out 8 hours a day," says Matt. "I have two little boys and my wife and a career. In the real world, you have to learn how to adapt and create a sustainable, healthy lifestyle."

TARA COSTA Season 7 Finalist

Starting Weight: 294

Finale Weight: 139

Today's Weight: 160

Tara Costa says she's discovered a whole new side of herself since she left the ranch. Living as a fast-paced city girl, she admits, "The smallest thing used to provoke me." But now, she says, "I've learned how to stop and breathe." As she became healthier and happier in her own life, she's developed a new sense of patience and a desire to help other people. Today, she's pursuing a master's degree in community health administration as well as a certification in life coaching.

"I definitely think patience is a learned thing," she reflects. "And now, because I know what it feels like to be overweight, I don't want anyone else to feel like I felt."

Tara won a record eight challenges during Season 7 and was known as one of the fiercest competitors in the house. The resolve she demonstrated on campus has continued in her life at home. Tara ran the New York City Marathon in 2009 and now participates in health fairs and community races across the country.

She continues to eat a wholesome diet full of fresh fruit, veggies, and lean protein. "But it's unrealistic to think you're never going to eat a treat again," she admits. She says she recently went into an ice cream shop to get a cone and was recognized by the server. "People are always watching what you eat. But the difference is I'm only having one cone, it's not an everyday thing, and I'm enjoying it. Everything in moderation."

For Tara, life today is sweet. "Everything is different—from the way I look at myself in the mirror to the way I feel about myself to the choices I make on a daily basis. I finally realized that I have a choice to make every day. Before, I was in a rut. I just thought, 'Well, this is the way it's going to be.' Now I realize I have a choice."

BERNIE SALAZAR Season 5 At-Home Winner

Starting Weight: 283

Finale Weight: 153

Today's Weight: 170

Bernie Salazar says he doesn't have a sweet *tooth*, he has a mouth full of sweet *teeth*. In fact, he may be the only contestant in *Biggest Loser* history to have a cupcake named after him. "If you're in Chicago, go to Sensational Bites," he says. "There's a cupcake in there I used to eat so much that now it's got my name, Bernie's Boston Cream Pie cupcake. Tell 'em to cut it in half for you so you can have half there and then take the rest home and share it."

That's the big difference in Bernie's life. He no longer eats the whole thing and no longer eats it every day. "I stay very conscious about my sweets. I used to be a sneaky snacker, but I refuse to do that anymore. I allow myself a treat every now and again, but I make an event of it. If I'm going to have something, it's going to be really good. I'm just going to have one, and I'm going to savor it. I don't wolf it down. I really enjoy the taste and feel satisfied after just one."

Another big difference in Bernie's life? He's now a married man—and his wife, Jennifer, is the cousin of his former teammate, Brittany Aberle. "Now, I'm technically Brittany's cousin!" he laughs. Brittany and Jennifer had actually applied for the show together, but it was Brittany who went on to be a cast member with Bernie. But Jennifer "kicked butt at home," says Bernie, and lost the weight on her own while her cousin was at the Ranch. Bernie says he and Jennifer met at a party after the show was done filming. "I completely lost my heart," he remembers. "And I was willing to lose it!"

Bernie was a teacher before going on *The Biggest Loser*, and education is still his passion, but his focus is now on health and wellness. He runs wellness workshops for kids and travels to schools to promote *Monstercize*, his children's book about exercise. "I really believe in this and have lots of faith in the message. I want to make the health of America's kids a priority."

DAN EVANS Season 5

Starting Weight: 310

Finale Weight: 174

Today's Weight: 190

America watched Dan Evans grow up on *The Biggest Loser*. He arrived on campus with his mom, Jackie, and left with a tattoo (courtesy of a trip to Las Vegas with teammates Mark Kruger and Roger Shultz) and the beginnings of a singing career. Today, his life is barreling along on all fronts. He stays physically active and performs with his band around the country.

"Most people go back home to their old environment," he says. "My challenge was new. I'm living the life that I always dreamed of but never actually experienced, which is living on a tour bus, playing in different cities every night. I needed to figure out how to live a reasonable, healthy life so that when people say, 'You're Dan from *The Biggest Loser*,' they can still say, 'You look great, and we're proud of you.'"

He figured out how to stay healthy on the road by realizing there are always healthy options available if he maps out a plan in advance. "I had to start planning. I can be on the road and make a healthy turkey sandwich. I can buy a bag of lettuce and whip up some salads, and it's just as quick and easy. I don't have to resort to a drive-thru."

Balance and moderation are a key part of his strategy for living healthy for many years to come. "This is forever," says Dan. "This is the rest of my life."

DANNY CAHILL Season 8 winner

Starting Weight: 430

Finale Weight: 191

Today's Weight: 205

Don't let the numbers fool you. Danny Cahill may weigh a few more pounds today than he did at the finale, but through ongoing hard workouts and strength training, he has packed on muscle, which takes up less space than fat, and is wearing a smaller pant size than he did at the finale. "I feel like I'm 20," says the 40-year-old. "I'm in better shape now than ever, and I'm more toned."

He's managing his weight in the real world by following what he calls the 80-20 rule. "Eighty percent of the time I eat healthy, and 20 percent of the time I eat what I want. Like Mexican food—I still eat it occasionally, but I don't eat all the cheese and chips anymore. I don't pig out. I eat my fill and really kill it in the gym the next day or the day before, because I plan my treats."

Danny faced one of his biggest challenges after having skin removal surgery several months ago. "I couldn't work out for a couple of months after. I gained back a little weight but it really showed me that exercise has to be a part of my daily routine. I work out every day for 30 to 40 minutes, and I make it a hard workout."

He ran the Boston Marathon last year and is training for the New York City Marathon next year. "I ran my first *Biggest Loser* marathon in 7 hours. I ran the Boston Marathon in 5, and I want to do New York in 4."

Danny says that these days, the word *quit* is not part of his vocabulary. "Don't ever quit going after something you really want. Look at me. I was 400 pounds and thought my life had passed me by. I didn't know I could do this. My confidence level is at an all-time high."

TRACEY YUKICH Season 8

Starting Weight: 250
Finale Weight: 132
Today's Weight: 136

Tracey Yukich was at the center of one of the most dramatic *Biggest Loser* moments ever. In the first episode's challenge, a mile run down the beach, Tracey collapsed and had to be flown to a hospital via helicopter. After a two-week stay, she returned to the Ranch ready to fight for her place there. "I knew I needed the opportunity. I was in a rut in my life, and I needed to focus on myself," says the mother of four.

Today, she's taking care of herself in a big way. She teaches classes at a local gym, including spinning—something she learned to love from *Biggest Loser* trainer Bob Harper.

She also enjoyed working with the show's nutritionist, Cheryl Forberg, and is taking steps to earn her nutrition degree. "Cheryl really inspired me," says Tracey. "She sat down with me, and we went over all the nutrition principles and calories in the foods I was eating. I think it's really empowering to be able to help people like that."

Tracey says she thinks it's especially important for women—who are so often caregivers for others—to take care of themselves. "Wives and mothers tend to forget themselves. We are the center of our families and we manage everything, but we never take the time to manage ourselves. You have to put yourself at the top of your list."

She runs a pretty healthy ship at home for her kids. "My kitchen is full of fresh fruit, so my kids always have choices for snacks. People may complain about the cost of fresh food, but I find I spend far less on whole food than I did on that packaged stuff I used to buy." She still loves her chocolate, so she keeps individual servings of dark chocolate chips in baggies for an occasional sweet snack.

Today, life for Tracey is better than ever. "This process was about finding myself again and living a life that I love," she says. "If you're tired of watching the same thing in your life, change the channel."

CHERYL GEORGE *Season 9*

Starting Weight: 227

Finale Weight: 151

Today's Weight: 168

Cheryl George arrived at the Ranch with her son Daris, who went on to become a Season 9 finalist. This Oklahoma wife and mother says that today she's happily settled back into a healthier version of her old life. Gone are the days of going out to lunch almost daily and chowing down on fried catfish, slaw, and hushpuppies or a giant taco salad with cheese and sour cream.

Now, she says, she plans what she's going to eat each day. "I pay a lot more attention to it. I pack up salads full of cucumbers, green peppers, and tomatoes with chicken. For snacks, I bring clementines and almonds."

Cheryl was a self-described chocoholic in the old days. And today, she still allows herself a daily treat. But now it's just one miniature piece of chocolate instead of one king-size candy bar. And if she feels like some ice cream, she doesn't deprive herself. But instead of a big bowlful, she measures out ½ cup. "It's all about portion sizes," she says.

She's pretty consistent about getting in her workout before she goes to work, sometimes with a videotape at home. "I'm learning that if I don't get it in before I go to work, chances are higher that I won't get to it later in the day. I'm on my feet all day at work, so I need to get that workout in first."

As for the scale, Cheryl says she likes to weigh herself every morning to stay on top of things. "I feel like a different person," she says. "I'm proud of what I see. This is something I wanted to do for 30 years, lose the weight, and I've done it."

She and her husband now choose more active ways to spend their free time—like going bowling or running in a 5-K—instead of sitting around at home and watching TV.

"I can do anything I set my mind to," says Cheryl, who turned 52 in October. "I don't want to set limits anymore. People tell me I look 10 years younger! The real me is coming back to what I was as a teenager. I was always fun before. Now I'm fun again!"

2

The Biggest Loser Plan

When the contestants arrive at *The Biggest Loser* Ranch full of nerves, they're always relieved to learn that they're going to be encouraged—of all things—to eat! Deprivation has no place in *The Biggest Loser* eating plan. From day one, nutritionist Cheryl Forberg and trainers Bob Harper and Jillian Michaels drill into the contestants that they need to eat quality calories throughout the day in order to keep their metabolisms burning and their blood sugar level stable and to be fueled for intense workouts.

Season 10's Aaron Thompkins says he was shocked to learn that he was supposed to eat every 4 hours. Before he came to *The Biggest Loser*, Aaron was a big consumer of low-quality calories. In fact, his favorite sandwich—which he ate a few times a week—was called the Terminator. It featured prime rib, cheese, and french fries piled high on a roll. He'd wolf down one and be uncomfortably stuffed for hours. But at the Ranch, he quickly realized how good it felt to satisfy his hunger with nutrient-dense, fresh, whole foods in the form of several meals and snacks throughout the day.

After they leave the Ranch, many contestants realize that even when they occasionally go overboard with their eating, they don't feel good the next day. "When you eat a bigger, richer meal," says Danny Cahill, Season 8's winner, "you feel a bit lethargic. Your body just feels so much better when you're eating clean, healthy foods."

So let's start with the first lesson the contestants learn in *The Biggest Loser* kitchen, where calories count: What exactly is a calorie?

Fueling Your Body with Quality Calories

A calorie is a measurement of how much energy the food you eat provides for your body. You need energy to fuel physical activity as well as all metabolic processes, from maintaining your heartbeat to healing a broken bone or building lean muscle mass. Only four components of the food you eat supply calories: protein and carbohydrates (4 calories per gram), alcohol (7 calories per gram), and fat (9 calories per gram). Vitamins, minerals, fiber, and water do not supply calories.

Keep in mind that the quality of your calories is just as important as the quantity of your calories. Some calories will fuel your workouts, keep you feeling full and satisfied, help boost your body's immune system, and protect you from disease. Other calories (often referred to as "empty calories") don't really provide any benefits—in fact, they can make you feel tired, sluggish, and hungrier than you were before you ate. *The Biggest Loser* plan will show you how to fuel your body with quality calories. When you give your body the nutrients and energy it needs, you will not only lose weight, you'll also feel better than ever.

The Biggest Loser plan helps you determine the exact daily calorie intake you require to meet your individual weight-loss goals. If you weigh 150 pounds or more, the simple calorie budget formula below, created by *The Biggest Loser* experts, will help you calculate how many calories you need each day. If you weigh less than 150 pounds, talk to your doctor about a calorie budget based on your individual weight-loss needs.

Calorie Budget Calculation

Your present weight × 7 = Your daily calorie needs for weight loss

As you lose weight, you'll need to continually reassess and reduce your calorie budget in order to keep losing weight and break through plateaus. If you've ever watched the show, you know that *The*

Jim Germanakos, Season 4 At-Home Winner

My father once said, "The only way to get it done . . . is to get it started." Anything is possible if you get it started. Set attainable goals and just get it done. Don't let anything or anybody stand between you and what's going to make you happy. You only live once. Make it the best life possible.

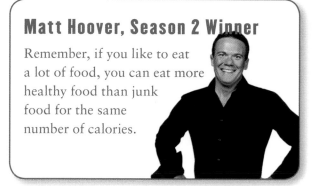

Matt Hoover, Season 2 Winner

Remember, if you like to eat a lot of food, you can eat more healthy food than junk food for the same number of calories.

Biggest Loser contestants lose a lot of weight during their first few weeks at the Ranch. But after they've been there for a while and have less weight to lose, they have to constantly increase the intensity of their workouts and be vigilant about tracking every calorie they consume to keep losing.

Age is another factor in weight loss. Our muscles burn a lot of calories each day—about 10 times as many as our fat tissue does. But muscles shrink with age, which means we have a natural tendency to burn fewer calories as we get older. So as our muscle mass decreases, our body fat increases. While you may lose weight more slowly as you get older, don't let that hold you back from your goals. Season 7's Estella Hayes has discovered to her delight that she has gained muscle since her time on the Ranch. "I'm a postmenopausal woman," she says. "But I've gained 15 pounds of lean body mass. Don't let them tell you that older women can't build muscle!"

Allocating Your Calories

Now that you've determined your daily calorie budget, the next step is to figure out how many calories to allocate for each meal and snack. On *The Biggest Loser* plan, you'll eat 3 meals and 2 snacks a day.

Divide your total daily calorie budget by four to determine how many calories you should spend on each meal and snack. The example below uses a sample calorie budget of 1,800—yours may be more or less, depending on your goal and starting weight.

Total daily calorie budget: 1,800
$$1{,}800 \div 4 = 450$$

So for each meal—breakfast, lunch, and dinner—this person has a 450-calorie budget.

Now divide the remaining one-fourth of your total daily calorie budget—in this case, 450—by two.

$$450 \div 2 = 225$$

So, for each of two daily snacks, this person has a 225-calorie budget.

This equation is just a starting point. Use it to help you determine a distribution of calories throughout the day that keeps you satisfied. If you go to the gym in the morning, for example, and require a bigger breakfast to fuel your workout, feel free to shift your calorie intake toward the start of your day. You can move your calorie distribution around to suit your needs and schedule.

If you prefer to eat several small meals throughout the day, you can do that, too. Six 300-calorie meals throughout the day is certainly an option for someone on an 1,800-calorie budget. Season 9's Cheryl George says she keeps most meals to 400 calories and under and snacks to 150 calories. "That's what works for me, so that's how I eat."

In order to accurately gauge the calorie content of your meals and snacks, you'll need to familiarize yourself with serving sizes. It's important to weigh and measure food so that you know exactly how many calories you're consuming. It's useful to have the following tools (many of which you may already own) to help you measure your portion sizes:

- Liquid measuring cup (2-cup capacity)
- Set of dry measuring cups (includes 1-cup, ½-cup, ⅓-cup, and ¼-cup sizes)
- Measuring spoons (1 tablespoon, 1 teaspoon, ½ teaspoon, and ¼ teaspoon)

- Food scale (such as *The Biggest Loser* Food Scale, available at online retailers)
- Calculator

Be sure that your food scale measures grams. (A gram is very small, about $\frac{1}{28}$ of an ounce.) Most of your weight measurements will be in ounces, but certain foods, such as nuts, are very concentrated in calories, so you may need to measure your portion size in grams. There is a wide range of food scales available these days.

A calculator will be indispensable for tallying your calories at the end of the day. It can also come in handy when the portion size of a food you want to eat differs from the suggested serving listed on its packaging. You may have to do a little math to figure out how many calories you're actually consuming.

When you're making your meals at home, be sure to weigh and measure your food *after* cooking. A food's weight can change dramatically when cooked. For example, 4 ounces of boneless skinless chicken breast has around 130 calories when raw. When it's cooked, it'll weigh closer to 3 ounces but will have nearly the same caloric content. The same holds true for vegetables and other cooked foods. Dry cereals or grains, on the other hand, can double or even triple in volume after being cooked with water. Remember that an ounce of weight is not the same as a fluid ounce. You can-

not convert the two without knowing the density of the ingredient you are measuring.

After precisely measuring your foods for a week or so, you'll be able to make fairly accurate estimates on your own. Over time, you'll know what right-size portions look like, whether you're cooking a meal in your own kitchen or deciding how much of your entrée to eat in a restaurant (and how much of it to wrap up and take home). But in the beginning, the tools mentioned above can help you get it just right. You can reference the conversion table on page 20 for a list of common measurements and conversions.

CONVERSION TABLE FOR MEASURING PORTION SIZES

Teaspoons	Tablespoons	Cups	Pints, quarts, gallons	Fluid ounces	Milliliters
¼ teaspoon					1 ml
½ teaspoon					2 ml
1 teaspoon	⅓ tablespoon				5 ml
3 teaspoons	1 tablespoon	¹⁄₁₆ cup		½ oz	15 ml
6 teaspoons	2 tablespoons	⅛ cup		1 oz	30 ml
12 teaspoons	4 tablespoons	¼ cup		2 oz	60 ml
16 teaspoons	5⅓ tablespoons	⅓ cup		2½ oz	75 ml
24 teaspoons	8 tablespoons	½ cup		4 oz	125 ml
32 teaspoons	10⅔ tablespoons	⅔ cup		5 oz	150 ml
36 teaspoons	12 tablespoons	¾ cup		6 oz	175 ml
48 teaspoons	16 tablespoons	1 cup	½ pint	8 oz	237 ml
		2 cups	1 pint	16 oz	473 ml
		3 cups		24 oz	710 ml
		4 cups	1 quart	32 oz	946 ml
		8 cups	½ gallon	64 oz	
		16 cups	1 gallon	128 oz	

The Biggest Loser Plan

The *Biggest Loser* nutrition pyramid is made up of fruits and vegetables at its base, protein foods on the second tier, and whole grains on the third tier. The top tier is a 200-calorie budget for healthy fats and "extras."

On *The Biggest Loser* 4-3-2-1 plan, you will eat a daily minimum of four servings of fruits and vegetables; up to three servings of healthy protein; up to two servings of whole grains; and up to one serving of "extras."

45 Percent of Your Daily Calories: Vegetables, Fruits, and Whole Grains

At the base of the pyramid, fruits and vegetables supply most of your daily nutrients in the form of vitamins, minerals, and fiber and contain relatively low numbers of calories. Aim for a minimum of 4 cups daily of a variety of fruits and nonstarchy vegetables. You can eat more than four servings a day of most fruits and vegetables if you wish, though the majority of your choices should be vegetables, which typically contain fewer calories than fruit.

THE 4-3-2-1 BIGGEST LOSER PYRAMID

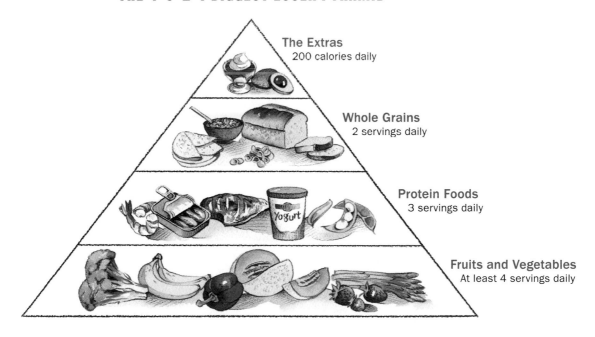

The Extras
200 calories daily

Whole Grains
2 servings daily

Protein Foods
3 servings daily

Fruits and Vegetables
At least 4 servings daily

Vegetables: Serving size = 1 cup or 8 ounces

Tips for Eating Vegetables:

- When cooking vegetables, avoid added fat; steam, grill, or stir-fry veggies in a nonstick pan with a spray (not a splash) of healthy oil.

- Try to eat at least one vegetable raw each day. Try a new vegetable each week so that you don't get bored with the same veggies.

- Eat a vegetable salad for lunch or dinner most days of the week.

- Keep precut vegetables such as bell peppers, celery, broccoli, and jicama in your fridge for easy snacking at home or to take to work or school.

- Starchier vegetables such as pumpkin, winter squash, and sweet potatoes are higher in calories and carbs, so limit them to one or two servings per week.

- Fresh vegetables are best, but you can choose frozen, as well. If you opt for canned, be sure to rinse contents before eating to wash away added salt.

Fruit: Serving size = 1 cup, 1 medium piece, or 8 ounces

Tips for Eating Fruit:

- Enjoy at least one whole fruit each day. Apples, oranges, pears, bananas, and grapes are all easily portable and can be eaten for snacks on the go.

- Dark green, light green, orange, purple, red, and yellow: Savor fruits from different color groups. This ensures you're getting a variety of nutrients.

- Eat fruit for sweet snacks and dessert. With just a little "fixing up," fresh and frozen fruit can be dessert stars. Try the Naked Apple Tart (page 44), Hot-to-Trot Honey Lime Melon Bowl (page 105), or Banana "Ice Cream" (page 112) for easy fruit treats.

- Opt for fresh fruit over dried fruits, which are more concentrated in calories and sugar and less filling.

- Choose whole fruit rather than fruit juices. Fruit juice contains less fiber, so it's not as filling as whole fruit, and it's more concentrated in sugars, so it will cause a spike in your blood sugar. When you do choose juice, keep in mind that a serving size is 4 ounces (½ cup).

Koli Palu, Season 9

When I'm traveling, I always pack a snack of an apple or orange and some almonds. And I make sure I have plenty of water, not soda.

- Fresh fruit is preferable, but frozen fruit is fine as long as it's not packaged with added sugar or syrup. If you choose canned fruit, be sure it's packed in water.

- Use fruit as a base for refreshing smoothies and shakes like the Monkey Shake (page 208) or the Can-Do Cranberry Orange Smoothie (page 211).

Whole Grains: Serving size = 1 cup of cooked grains or 2 slices of bread

Choose whole grain foods in moderation and be sure to read labels and select those with high fiber content. On *The Biggest Loser* plan, you will eat two servings of whole grains daily.

When grains are refined, important nutrients are removed. All that's usually left is starch, which is loaded with carbohydrate calories and little else. *Whole grains* undergo minimal processing and thus retain most of their nutritional value. The whole grain family includes barley, corn, oats, quinoa, rice, and wheat. These are all great sources of protein, B vitamins, antioxidants, and fiber.

Tips for Eating Whole Grains:

- When choosing bread products, read the label carefully. If it says "enriched," the product probably contains white flour—meaning it's low in fiber and nutrition.

- Choose breads with at least 2 grams of fiber per serving, but aim for 5 grams. When you read the ingredient list, look for "whole wheat" or "whole grain" among the first few ingredients. "Wheat flour" isn't necessarily whole wheat.

- Most packaged breakfast cereals are highly processed and loaded with added sugar. Choose cereals with fewer than 5 grams of sugar and at least 5 grams of fiber per serving.

- White flour, white sugar, white bread, and packaged baked goods affect your blood sugar and insulin too quickly—you don't want an excess of either in your bloodstream. And unlike their whole grain counterparts, these foods also lack antioxidants and fiber. Choose whole grains that will keep you feeling fuller longer.

30 Percent of Your Daily Calories: Protein

Protein is a macronutrient found in meat, fish, eggs, poultry, and dairy products, and in smaller amounts in beans, nuts, and whole grains. Protein is required to build and repair muscle, skin, hair, blood vessels, and other bodily tissues. Generally speaking, any food containing at least 9 grams of protein per serving is a high-protein food.

Lean proteins contain valuable nutrients that can help you achieve a healthy weight. Be sure to include protein with each meal and each snack so your body can benefit from it all day long. When you haven't eaten enough protein, you might find yourself running low on energy or suffering from muscle fatigue. Try to eat a little bit of protein or drink a protein shake within 30 minutes after a workout to help your muscles repair. In addition to helping build muscle, protein also promotes the feeling of satiety, or fullness, thus curbing your appetite and keeping you from consuming extra calories. When combined with a carbohydrate (such as a piece of fruit), protein helps slow the release of blood sugar, sustaining your energy for longer periods of time.

Choose a variety of proteins to make up your three daily servings. Try to limit consumption of lean red meat to twice a week, and avoid processed meats such as bologna, hot dogs, and sausage, which are typically high in sodium and contain nitrates. Fish is an excellent source of protein, omega-3 fatty acids, vitamin E, and selenium.

To figure out how many grams of protein should constitute each of your three daily servings, use the formula below, which uses an 1,800-calorie budget as an example.

$$1,800 \times 0.30 = 540 \text{ calories from protein}$$

Then convert the calories to grams.

$$540 \div 4 \text{ calories per gram} = 135 \text{ grams of protein}$$

You can then allocate protein goals for each meal and snack, based on your total daily protein intake. Using the example above, daily protein servings might look like this:

Breakfast: 33 grams

Snack 1: 17 grams

Lunch: 34 grams

Snack 2: 17 grams

Dinner: 34 grams

Animal Protein: Serving size = 1 cup or 8 ounces
Meat
Choose lean cuts of meat, such as pork tenderloin and beef round, chuck, sirloin, or tenderloin. USDA Choice or USDA Select grades of beef usu-

Nicole Michalik, Season 4

Share, share, share! When I go out to dinner with my friends, we get a dessert to share. We each get about three forkfuls, and it's more than enough to satisfy our afterdinner sweet tooth. Most of the time, you think you want more dessert than you really need to be satisfied.

ally have lower fat content. Avoid meat that is heavily marbled and remove any visible fat. Try to find ground meat that is at least 95 percent lean.

Poultry

The leanest poultry is the skinless white meat from the breast of chicken or turkey. When purchasing ground chicken or turkey, ask for the white meat.

Seafood

Seafood is an excellent source of protein, omega-3 fatty acids, vitamin E, and selenium. When you're buying seafood, go for options that are rich in omega-3 fatty acids, such as herring, mackerel, salmon, sardines (water packed), trout, and tuna.

Dairy: Serving size = 1 cup or 8 ounces

Top choices include fat-free (skim) milk, 1 percent (low-fat) milk, buttermilk, plain fat-free or low-fat yogurt, fat-free or low-fat yogurt with fruit (no sugar added), fat-free or low-fat cottage cheese, and fat-free or low-fat ricotta cheese. Light soy milks and soy yogurts are also fine, but if you eat soy because of a dairy intolerance or allergy, be sure to select soy products that are fortified with calcium. Egg whites are another excellent source of fat-free protein.

If you're not eating three servings of dairy per day, *The Biggest Loser* nutrition team recommends that you consider taking a calcium supplement.

Vegetarian Protein: Serving size = 1 cup or 8 ounces

Good sources of vegetarian protein include beans, nuts and seeds, and traditional soy foods, such as tofu and edamame. Many of these foods are also loaded with fiber.

25 Percent of Your Daily Calories: Good Fats

Healthy fats play a role in weight loss because they help you feel full and satisfied. But remember: Even good fats are a concentrated source of calories, and as such, you need to monitor your serving sizes carefully. Many of your fat calories will be hidden in your carbohydrate and protein food choices. You will have a small budget of leftover calories to spend on healthy fat and "extras"—like desserts and sweet snacks.

Fats should make up no more than 25 percent of your total daily calories, and saturated fats should account for no more than 10 percent of your daily calorie budget. Here's how to calculate your daily fat intake, again based on the example of an 1,800-calorie budget.

Multiply your total daily calorie budget by 0.25 to see how many calories can come from fat.

$$1,800 \times 0.25 = 450$$

So up to 450 of this person's daily calories may come from fat.

One gram of fat contains 9 calories. So simply divide the number of calories from fat that you're allotted each day (in this case, 450) by nine.

$$450 \div 9 = 50$$

A person with an 1,800-calorie budget would consume no more than 50 grams of fat daily.

Tips for Eating Healthy Fats:

- Choose olive oil, canola oil, flaxseed oil, or walnut oil for salads, cooking, and baking.

- When adding fat to a sandwich, try using reduced-fat mayonnaise or a little mashed-up avocado.

- Snack on nuts and seeds in moderation. Nut butters, trail mix, and raw nuts pack a powerful energy punch and supply a good dose of unsaturated fat. Keep portion sizes moderate; for example, 14 walnut halves make a 1-ounce serving.

- Choose unsaturated fats. Many unsaturated fats, classified as monounsaturated or polyunsaturated, can lower your LDL cholesterol (bad) and raise your HDL (good) cholesterol.

- Avoid trans fat, which is an artificial fat found in hard margarines and vegetable shortenings, packaged baked goods, and foods fried in hydrogenated fat. Carefully read labels of packaged foods. If you see the words *hydrogenated* or *partially hydrogenated*, put the package back on the shelf.

Decoding Food Packaging

Keeping a food journal will require you to become an expert at reading food labels and Nutrition Facts panels. When you're shopping for healthy foods, labels can help you choose between similar products based on calorie and nutrient (such as fat, protein, or fiber) content.

The label on the opposite page is an example

Nutrition Facts

Serving Size
Servings Per Container

Amount Per Serving

Calories 0   Calories from Fat 0

% Daily Value*

Total Fat 0g	0%
Saturated Fat 0g	0%
Trans Fat 0g	
Cholesterol 0mg	0%
Sodium 0mg	0%
Total Carbohydrate 0g	0%
Dietary Fiber 0g	0%
Soluble Fiber 0g	0%
Insoluble Fiber 0g	0%
Sugars 0g	
Protein 0g	

Vitamin A 0%	•	Vitamin C 0%	
Calcium 0%	•	Iron 0%	
Phosphorus 0%	•	Magnesium 0%	

* Percent Daily Values are based on a 2,000 calorie diet. Your daily values may be higher or lower depending on your calorie needs:

		Calories:	2,000	2,500
Total Fat	Less than		0g	0g
Sat Fat	Less than		0g	0g
Cholesterol	Less than		0mg	0mg
Sodium	Less than		0mg	0mg
Potassium			0mg	0mg
Total Carbohydrate			0g	0g
Dietary Fiber			0g	0g

Calories per gram:
Fat 0   •   Carbohydrate 0   •   Protein 0

INGREDIENTS: Whole Wheat Flour, (Stone Ground Whole Oats, Hard Red Winter Wheat, Rye, Long Grain Brown Rice, Triticale, Buckwheat, Barley, Sesame Seeds), Malted Barley, Salt, Yeast, Mixed Tocopherols (Natural Vitamin E) for Freshness.

---

of what you'll find on the packaging of any item at your local supermarket. It contains a lot of information, but here is a list of what you most need to evaluate how to make healthy choices.

Serving size: Everything else on the label (calories, grams of fat, etc.) is based on this measurement. Just because a food label suggests a certain portion doesn't mean that it's the right serving size for you. Look at the calorie and fat content that corresponds to the serving size. If you need to, cut the serving size in half.

Calories: This lists calories per serving. Be sure that the number of calories you record in your food journal reflects the number of calories you've eaten. If the label indicates that a serving is 1 cup and you ate 2 cups, you need to double the calories you record in your journal to match your double serving.

Total fat: The number of fat grams in a product reflects the sum of three kinds of fat: saturated fat, polyunsaturated fat, and monounsaturated fat. Pay special attention to the numbers of calories on "light," reduced-fat, low-fat, and fat-free products. When the fat is removed from many recipes, salt or sugar is sometimes added to enhance the flavor. This can result in a fat-free or low-fat product that actually contains more calories than the regular version.

Saturated fat: Less than one-third of your daily fat grams should come from saturated fats, which are derived mainly from animal products and are solid at room temperature (such as butter and shortening). Some plant oils, such as coconut oil and palm oil, also contain saturated fats. The saturated fat from animal foods is the primary source of cholesterol.

Sodium: For most people, the daily recommended sodium intake is no more than 2,400 milligrams. Some of the foods you eat each day will have more, others less. Aim for an average of no more than 240 milligrams of sodium in each meal or snack.

Total carbohydrate: This number is calculated by adding grams of complex carbohydrates plus grams of fiber plus grams of sugars. If the total carbohydrate number is more than double the amount of sugars, that means there are more "good carbs" than "bad carbs" in the food.

Dietary fiber: Fiber is found in plant foods but not in animal foods. Unless you're on a fiber-restricted diet, aim for at least 25 to 35 grams of fiber per day.

Sugars: The sugars in a food can be naturally occurring or added. Check the ingredient list to find out, and avoid eating foods that contain processed sugars, such as high-fructose corn syrup. The total grams of carbohydrates in a food serving should be more than twice the number of grams of sugar.

Protein: If a food has more than 9 grams of protein per serving, it's considered a high-protein food. It's important to eat foods that are high in protein when you're trying to lose weight because protein is a great source of energy and helps you feel full.

Ingredient list: A product's ingredients are listed in order of decreasing weight. If the first few ingredients listed include any form of sugar (cane sugar, corn syrup, sucrose, and so on) or fats and oils, the food is probably not a good choice for weight loss. Also, look for products with a short list of ingredients you recognize. A long list of strange-sounding ingredients is always a red flag. Leave those products on the shelf at the grocery store—don't put them on the shelf of your pantry.

Structuring Your Day

As you already know, on *The Biggest Loser* plan, you'll eat three meals (breakfast, lunch, and dinner) and two snacks a day. Parceling out your calories throughout the day means you'll stay full and won't go on sugar or carb binges to satisfy your growling stomach. It also means you won't go to bed feeling stuffed and sick from too many bad, empty calories. "It was amazing, being in the kitchen with Bob and Jillian our first day and learning that eating is okay," says Season 10 contestant Adam Hurtado. "I found out it's not good to starve myself at breakfast. It's only going to lead up to a big binge later in the day, and that's something I had been doing before I got to the Ranch."

Eating more-frequent meals and snacks will:

- Keep you from feeling deprived
- Help control blood sugar and insulin levels (insulin is a fat-forming hormone)
- Lead to lower body fat
- Keep you energized for exercise and activity

- Reduce stress hormones in the body that can contribute to fat accumulation
- Establish a regular pattern of eating that helps prevent impulse eating

"At first, I really had to work to get all my meals in," recalls Season 8 winner Danny Cahill. "I wasn't used to eating healthy. I quickly realized that nutrient-dense foods were more satisfying than all the fat I was getting from fast food. It kept up my energy level, and I felt fueled for workouts."

Contestants are often surprised to learn that their past habit of skipping meals contributed to their weight gain. The problem with skipping meals is that by the time the next mealtime rolls around, you're famished and more likely to choose the wrong foods, especially those high in fat. Fat has more than twice as many calories as protein and carbohydrate. It satisfies hunger very quickly, and your body seems to know this. So the longer you go without food, the more likely you are to crave a high-fat treat.

The other problem with skipping meals is that when you wait too long to eat, you lose sight of your body's natural hunger cues. You don't really know when you're hungry anymore (or when you're full). Most overeaters don't stop eating when they're full—they stop when they're stuffed!

From starving to stuffed, the hunger scale

The Biggest Loser Hunger Scale

1. **Famished or starving:** You feel weak and/or lightheaded. This is a big no-no.

2. **Very hungry:** You can't think of anything else but eating. You're cranky and irritable and can't concentrate.

3. **Hungry:** Your stomach's growling and feels empty.

4. **A little bit hungry:** You're just starting to think about your next meal.

5. **Satisfied:** You're comfortable, not really thinking about food. You feel alert and have a good energy level.

6. **Fully satisfied:** You've had enough to eat, maybe a little too much. Maybe you took a few extra bites for taste only, not hunger.

7. **Very full:** Now you need to unzip your jeans. You're uncomfortable, bloated, tired. Maybe you don't feel great. Where's the couch . . . ? You should never feel like this after a meal.

Hunger Scale Flash Card

1–3: Eat! Eat!

5: Stop, especially if you're trying to lose weight.

6: Definitely stop.

7: You may have waited too long. Better go find the couch and start over tomorrow.

If your hunger is anywhere from level 1 through 3, you should eat.

If you're at level 4, drink a glass of water, chew a piece of sugar-free gum, or do something else to distract yourself from thinking about food.

When you're trying to lose weight, you should try to stop eating when you reach level 5, but definitely no later than level 6. If you get to level 7, you've eaten too much. Anything above that is way too much and will sabotage your weight-loss efforts.

If you're not in the habit of eating regular meals and snacks, creating a food schedule that you use in conjunction with a daily food journal can help you stay on track. Successful *Biggest Losers* learn over time that carefully planning and recording their meals and snacks is one of the most important components of successful weight loss and maintenance.

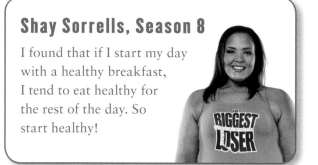

Shay Sorrells, Season 8

I found that if I start my day with a healthy breakfast, I tend to eat healthy for the rest of the day. So start healthy!

on the opposite page defines your body's hunger signals and how to interpret them.

Planning Regular Meals and Snacks

Trainer Jillian Michaels has a saying that usually catches on among each season's contestants: "If you fail to plan, you plan to fail." Planning is crucial to just about every aspect of weight loss, from planning meals and snacks to planning exercise and adequate sleep. Part of planning includes making sure you have your food journal with you at all times to record every meal and snack. Tara Costa of Season 7 says planning is the one crucial thing all former contestants have to do. "If you stop planning your meals, the weight can sneak back on. I recently took a vacation, and I packed a cooler of healthy snacks for the drive," she said, knowing that the rest stops she'd face on her road trip would offer limited options.

Breakfast

When it comes to breakfast, rule number one is: Eat it every day, no skipping. If you're not used to eating something within an hour of waking up, you'll have to teach your body to re-cue its hunger signals. Try starting small and eating something simple, such as a bowl of fruit or a slice of whole grain toast with some almond butter. Try to include fiber and protein in your breakfast, which will keep you feeling full all morning. Lots of contestants learn that a quick breakfast of Greek yogurt, fruit, and whole grain cereal is a good first meal for the day, and it only take minutes to prepare.

Lunch

It's easy to eat fast food in the car, buy lunch from a vending machine, or grab a handful of something from the fridge. But you'll probably make better food choices—and enjoy your meal more—if you do a little prep work ahead of time and use lunch as an opportunity to recharge for the second half of your day. As trainer Jillian Michaels points out, fueling your body with healthy food in the middle of the day will keep your metabolism on an even keel.

Make sure your lunch includes a combination of lean protein, complex carbs, and healthy fats. You might have a salad with lots of vegetables and a serving of lean protein, or a sandwich made with whole grain bread. You've got a lot to accomplish in your afternoon, so feed yourself wisely! "Sometimes the simplest things are delicious," says Season 10's Lisa Mosely, who has discovered a new lunch favorite: lean roasted turkey wrapped in fresh, crisp leaves of romaine lettuce. "It's quick and healthy, so there goes my excuse about not having enough time to make a healthy lunch," the single mother of two admits.

Snacks

Snacks should be eaten mid-morning and mid-afternoon, a few hours after you've eaten breakfast or lunch, when you're beginning to feel your energy

wane. Try to eat something about every 3 to 4 hours, which will help keep cravings at bay, blood sugar stable, and your energy up. Aim for a snack that combines one serving of carbohydrates (such as a piece of whole fruit) with a half serving of protein (such as a low-fat cheese stick). Protein will help you feel full and satisfied, and when combined with carbs, a snack will help keep your blood sugar stable.

When you're away from home, be sure to plan and pack your snacks for the day. Many *Biggest Losers* also find it helpful to keep preportioned snacks in the fridge in plastic bags or reusable containers—they're handy for preworkout pick-me-ups and postgym refueling. "You have to keep your metabolism going," advises Season 10 contestant Alfredo Dintem. "I had never thought of it like that before, but I do now."

Dinner

Take the time to slow down and enjoy your dinner. Write down your shopping list over the weekend and make a supermarket run to ensure you stock your kitchen for the busy week ahead. Try to cook a few healthy meals on the weekend that you can refrigerate or freeze in individual portions and heat up as needed for a quick weeknight meal. Plan your weekly menu based on your calorie budget and weight-loss goals.

Dinner doesn't have to be a big, heavy meal. In

fact, for most contestants, dinner turns out to be the lightest meal of all. "Lean and green all the way" is how Season 10's Ada Wong describes her dinners at the Ranch. "I make a big salad with mixed greens, bell peppers, mushrooms, tuna or turkey, and balsamic vinegar or salsa as dressing." Most contestants also avoid eating lots of carbs at night. "No more steak and potatoes for me at night," says Jesse Atkins, also of Season 10. "At the end of the day, a lot of food is just going to sit in your stomach and end up on your butt or on your thighs!"

Liquid Calories

Your beverage of choice should always be water. If you're not already doing so, make sure to drink eight 8-ounce glasses of water a day to stay properly hydrated. This is especially important when you're changing your food habits and incorporating more fiber into your diet. Record your water intake in your journal each day to be sure you've met your quota.

Staying hydrated improves all bodily functions at the cellular level and helps your heart and kidneys work more efficiently. In addition, water carries glucose, nutrients, and dietary antioxidants to your tissues, resulting in an energy boost and other health benefits. And water actually helps regulate body temperature (especially important for people with poor circulation) and helps you feel full. In

Cheryl George, Season 9
When you're working out hard, you need to fuel your body. Give it the nutrition it needs to do what you want it to do.

fact, some studies have shown that drinking a large glass of water 30 minutes before a meal can help reduce calorie intake during the meal.

In addition to water, coffee, tea, low-fat or skim milk, and protein shakes are other acceptable beverages on *The Biggest Loser* plan. Try to limit caffeine consumption to a minimum, however, and if you're drinking coffee or tea, it should never include syrup, whipped cream, or chocolate! Choose low-calorie beverages such as unsweetened green tea and record them in your journal.

Biggest Loser nutritionist Cheryl Forberg, RD, is still amazed by how many contestant hopefuls come to her with a daily six-pack soda habit, taking in almost as many calories as they need in a day just swigging the stuff. If you're craving a sweet drink, try one of the Sweet Sips in Chapter 9 instead of choosing high-calorie, high-sugar sodas.

Another source of liquid calories for many *Biggest Losers* before they arrive at the Ranch is alcohol. Beer, wine, and cocktail calories add up quickly, and the more alcoholic beverages you drink, the more likely you are to have lowered inhibitions—and drink and eat even more. Chef Devin Alexander says she loves to have a good cocktail every now and then, so she makes them as low-cal as possible and adds fruit to the mix to boost the quality of the calories and create something truly special. Her Frozen Blueberry Margarita (page 198) is sure to make an impression at any special occasion, from cocktail parties to picnics.

Get Moving

As you know by now, weight loss is all about calories in and calories out. Calculating a calorie budget, planning your meals and snacks, and tracking what you eat in a food journal are all great ways to make sure you are taking in the right number and right kind of calories. But what about that "calories out" part of the equation?

The contestants at the Ranch put in long, hard workouts every day. But you don't have to work out for hours with Bob and Jillian to see results. If you're not already active, start incorporating more activity into your day. Walk or bike instead of driving; take the stairs instead of the elevator; treat your dog to an extra-long walk. It doesn't matter how small you start—you just have to get moving.

Andrea Hough, Season 9

Now I make time for workouts, getting up early and hitting the gym first. You only have so much time in your day to do things and you have to make working out a priority. You may have to sacrifice some TV time to do it.

"You don't need a lot of money to get healthy," says Season 10 contestant Sophia Franklin, who plans on bringing back a healthy lifestyle to her Maryland community. "You don't need a gym to walk outdoors. And everyone has a floor where they can do crunches or pushups."

If you already exercise moderately, consider increasing the duration (amount of time) you exercise and the intensity (how hard you exercise) to see more results. If you typically walk or run on a treadmill for 30 minutes, try adding an incline, holding some hand weights, or increasing your time by 10 minutes. If you take a beginner's yoga class once a week, ask yourself if you're ready to move to the intermediate level, or take the class twice week. The more you put into your fitness regimen, the more you will get out of it.

Here are some tools to help you get moving, no matter what your fitness level is today.

Make a Plan

Studies show that people who plan ahead for their workouts are generally more successful than those who wing it. Decide when you want to work out and put it in your day planner. Log that time as yours. After you've exercised, record your accomplishments in this journal.

- Set an alarm as a reminder to work out. Or schedule a reminder on your computer if that's where you spend most of your day.
- Pack your gym bag the night before so that you can grab it and go in the morning.

The wonderful thing is you'll discover that after awhile, you no longer have to hit the snooze bar repeatedly to get yourself on your feet. SunShine Hampton of Season 9 was amazed to find that after she returned home from the Ranch, she was waking up *before* her alarm clock went off, ready to go out for her walk and see what the day held for her.

Build a Team

At the Ranch, contestants are divided into teams to provide support and guidance for one another. You'll need that encouragement, too!

- Plan walking activities with your kids or encourage a friend to become an exercise buddy.
- Look for workout partners online through sites like biggestloserclub.com or through your local colleges, churches, and community centers.

Many contestants come to the Ranch having never experienced the benefits of a robust support system at home and quickly discover how helpful it is to have a team to cheer them on. Even in her early days at the Ranch, said Season 10 contestant Jessica Delfs, she found the support offered from her castmates invaluable.

"You're not a pawn in a game," she says. "You learn how to talk about things, discover that someone else might have a very similar story to you. When you share your struggles, you

Biggest Loser Trainer Tip: Bob Harper

Take little steps; do things you can easily manage. This will give you a sense of accomplishment that will make you come back for more.

might find common ground with someone. It helps you to start losing weight and get on with your life."

Be Consistent

Experts suggest that it takes 21 days of consistent behavior to form a habit—so don't get discouraged after only a couple of days. Find small ways to stay active, and before you know it, your body will start to crave exercise.

Get FITTE

FITTE is a quick, handy acronym to help you remember all the elements of an exercise routine you need to improve your fitness. It's a good way, especially for beginners, to start thinking about working out. As you begin to make exercise a part of your lifestyle, you'll want to vary or increase some or all elements of the FITTE principle:

Frequency: How often you work out

Intensity: How hard you work out (measuring with a heart rate monitor or using rate of perceived exertion)

Time: The duration of your workout

Type: The kind of exercise you're doing

Enjoyment: How much pleasure you get out of the activity

Frequency

The American Council on Exercise recommends 20 to 30 minutes of cardiovascular exercise 3 to 5 days a week (depending on intensity; a shorter workout duration calls for more intensity) and strength training at least twice a week. You can combine cardio and strength on some days or keep them separate.

Intensity: Load, Speed, and Effort

There are many ways to increase or decrease intensity.

- **Load:** This is the amount of resistance you use in your workout. For strength training, you can use your own body weight as resistance or increase the load (and intensity) by adding weights.

- **Speed:** During your cardio workouts, you can amp up intensity by simply going faster. It will help you burn more calories and strengthen your heart. You can vary speed in the strength exercises, too. When exercising with dumbbells, keep your speed under control to ensure that you never swing the weights.

- **Effort:** How hard are you working? One way to measure intensity is by using the rate of perceived exertion (RPE) scale, an easy-to-follow self-measurement. Use the rating scale on this page to gauge how your body feels when you're working out. RPE ranges from 6 (no exertion at all) to 20 (maximal exertion).

RATE OF PERCEIVED EXERTION SCALE

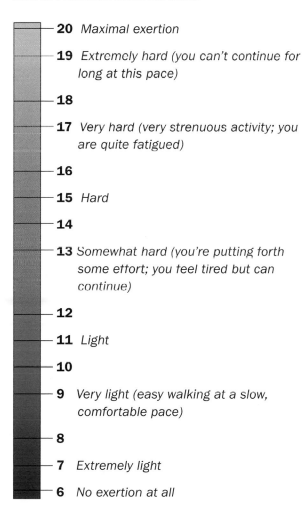

20 *Maximal exertion*

19 *Extremely hard (you can't continue for long at this pace)*

18

17 *Very hard (very strenuous activity; you are quite fatigued)*

16

15 *Hard*

14

13 *Somewhat hard (you're putting forth some effort; you feel tired but can continue)*

12

11 *Light*

10

9 *Very light (easy walking at a slow, comfortable pace)*

8

7 *Extremely light*

6 *No exertion at all*

Calculating Your Target Heart Rate

The rate of perceived exertion scale relates to your exercise heart rate as well. We all have a resting heart rate (our pulse rate when we are immobile), a maximum heart rate (the highest rate we should reach in a workout), and a target heart rate zone (for maximum fat burning). Your target heart rate—the rate that you should aim to achieve in your workouts—can be easily calculated, once you know your maximum heart rate. To find your maximum heart rate, follow this simple formula:

220 – your age = Maximum heart rate

So, for a 35-year-old, the maximum heart rate is 185 (220 – 35 = 185).

Now, to find your target heart rate zone, you're going to use the number you just calculated for your maximum heart rate:

Low-range target heart rate = Maximum heart rate × 0.80

High-range target heart rate = Maximum heart rate × 0.85

So, for the same 35-year-old…

- The target heart rate (low range) would be 148 (185 × 80% = 148).

- The target heart rate (high range) would be 157 (185 × 85% = 157).

This person should aim to keep his or her heart rate between 148 and 157 when exercising.

Studies have shown a correlation between rate of perceived exertion and heart rate, with heart rate equaling about 10 times the RPE you've reached. For example, if you're working out at an 11 on the scale, your heart rate should be approximately 110. For the 35-year-old, for example, this would not be in the target heart rate zone. He or she would need to increase the intensity and be more in the 14-to-16 range to achieve the 148-to-157 target heart rate zone. Looking at the RPE scale, this makes sense, as that range represents "somewhat hard" to "hard."

Phillip Parham, Season 6

I can do things now I couldn't do before, and I relish my victories. I try not to think too much about my setbacks. I encourage you to listen to your self-talk. You can be your greatest advocate *or* your worst enemy.

Time

Time (or duration) is how long you actually exercise. We're all challenged to find time to exercise, but it's important to stick to your exercise schedule and put in as many minutes or hours as you can dedicate if you want to achieve your weight-loss goals.

Type

The type of exercise you choose will have a great impact on whether you can maintain a fitness program. If you prefer, fulfill your 30 minutes of aerobic exercise with cycling rather than walking. Studies show that you'll be more likely to stick to an exercise program if you like what you're doing. Other options are swimming, jumping rope, and aerobics classes. If you don't enjoy lifting dumbbells, try using tubing, elastic bands, medicine balls, weighted water balls, or stability balls (go to biggestloser.com for products).

Enjoyment

It's important to create an exercise routine that you actually enjoy doing—that way, you're much more likely to stick with it. Season 9 champion Michael Ventrella used to hate exercising but says he actually looks forward to it these days. "I've become a much more active person. I'll hop on the elliptical in my house for 2 hours. I'll take my mountain bike and ride 20 to 30 miles on a bike path. It feels like second nature to me now."

3

A Passion for Fruit

Fruit is a wonderful thing for the *Biggest Losers*. Once they've given up the intense flavors of salty fast foods and overly sweet processed junk, they fall in love with the luscious flavor of fruit. Unadorned, fruit holds plenty of appeal, and many contestants count a fruit as their favorite go-to snack. But with just a little extra effort, even the most basic piece of fruit can be made into something special.

One way to bring out the natural sweetness of fruit is to bake it in the oven. Chef Devin Alexander says that she couldn't believe how delicious and sweet grapefruit became when she baked it for her Meringue-Topped Pink Grapefruit (page 51). "It is really killer," she promises.

Jessica Delfs of Season 10 makes a simple baked apple when she's looking for an easy dessert. "I use a melon baller and core out the stem area, making a little well," she says. "Then I crush up a couple of walnuts or almonds, add a dash of cinnamon or nutmeg and just 1 teaspoon of brown sugar. I add that to the well of the apple and drizzle 1 teaspoon of maple syrup over the top. Bake it at 400°F for 15 to 20 minutes." Sometimes she adds a tiny bit of apple juice at the bottom of the baking dish to create steam and help the apple soften. Who needs apple pie?

Another way to increase the sweetness of fresh fruit is to cut it up and let the juices seep out for a little while, which makes the fruit a bit softer and creates a natural syrup. Richard deRoque of Season 10 says he cuts up fruit in the evening and lets it sit in the fridge overnight. "I slice strawberries and sprinkle on some Truvia, then store them in a resealable container that I take with me to work. When I get a craving for a sweet snack, I have some strawberries, and it helps me get through the day."

Freezing fruit is another way to create different flavors and textures. Contestants often stash frozen grapes in zip-top baggies and pop a few into their mouths for a refreshing post-workout treat. Tara Costa of Season 7 says she hates the process of chopping up fresh fruit, so she stocks up on frozen favorites from the grocery store, like bags of frozen mango chunks, blueberries, pineapple, strawberries, and mixed berries. She combines all of the frozen fruit in a big bowl and just lets it defrost in the fridge. It's her favorite potluck supper contribution to take to a friend's dinner party. "If you want to get a little crazy," she says, "add some frozen yogurt, just one scoop." Keeping frozen berries on hand is also a great way to save money and ensure that you always have fruit at home. And they're perfect for making smoothies.

Whether you enjoy your fruit baked, chopped, fresh, or frozen, the fruit-forward desserts in the pages that follow are sure to please your palate without packing on extra pounds.

Biggest Loser Trainer Tip: Bob Harper

Every single season, these contestants inspire me. I look at all these contestants on our show throughout the years, and I just want say to the people sitting at home, what is *really* stopping you? What are you waiting for?

AMARETTO PEARS WITH TOASTED ALMONDS

Agave nectar has become increasingly popular in recent years as a substitute for corn syrup and other refined sweeteners. Its lower glycemic index value means that it doesn't create spikes in blood sugar the way that white sugar does. Recently it's become available in a number of flavored varieties. I particularly love the Irish crème and amaretto flavors, which can add a dash of low-cal and "virgin" flavor to dishes that would otherwise contain alcohol, such as these nutty Amaretto Pears.

Butter-flavored cooking spray

2 firm medium pears (any variety)

½ tablespoon unsalted butter, melted

1 tablespoon + 1 teaspoon amaretto-flavored agave nectar

4 lightly salted dry-roasted almonds, finely chopped

Preheat the oven to 375°F. Line an 8" × 8" baking dish with parchment paper (see page xiii). Lightly mist the parchment with cooking spray. Crinkle a large piece of foil to form a log about 6" long, 2" wide, and 1" high. Set the log in the center of the baking dish (this will ensure the pears lay flat so the glaze doesn't drip off during baking).

Cut the pears in half lengthwise. Carefully scoop out the cores and remove the stems. Place the halves on the prepared baking dish, cut sides up, so the tips rest on the prepared log. Drizzle the butter, then the agave evenly over the pear halves. Sprinkle the almonds evenly over the pears.

Bake for 55 to 60 minutes, or until very tender and lightly browned around the edges (you should be able to cut the pears with a fork without much muscle). Allow the pears to cool for 15 minutes, or until they're just warm or at room temperature. Serve.

Makes 4 servings

Per serving: 89 calories, <1 g protein, 18 g carbohydrates (14 g sugar), 2 g fat, <1 g saturated fat, 4 mg cholesterol, 2 g fiber, 2 mg sodium

NAKED APPLE TART

In culinary school, I used to make a tart very similar to this one, only it had a crust with enough butter to require a week of butt-kicking with Jillian! Now, I enjoy it naked—without a crust, that is.

I prefer the look of this "tart" when it's baked in a round or oval dish. You can use a similar-size square or rectangle dish, if necessary. Note that the tart cooks for quite a while, allowing the apples to transform into layers of soft, sweet deliciousness. The top of the tart will start to look burnt, but don't worry, it's not! It's just the result of juice and cinnamon caramelizing onto the apples—oh so sweet!

Butter-flavored cooking spray

2 large crisp apples (such as Golden Delicious or Granny Smith), peeled

¾ cup 100% apple juice (not from concentrate)

2 tablespoons coconut sugar

2 teaspoons unsalted butter, melted

1 teaspoon ground cinnamon

Preheat the oven to 425°F. Lightly mist a 10" ceramic or glass tart dish with cooking spray.

Cut the apples in half lengthwise and remove the cores. Slice each half lengthwise into very thin slices. Starting from the outer edges of the dish, arrange the apple slices, laying them horizontally, in tightly overlapping circles in the bottom of the dish, until all of the apple slices are used (they will make a rose or flower blossom pattern).

In a small mixing bowl, whisk together the apple juice, sugar, butter, and cinnamon until well combined (the sugar and cinnamon will not dissolve completely). Pour half of the apple juice mixture evenly over the apples. Reserve the remaining half.

Bake for 30 minutes. Pour the reserved mixture evenly over the apples. Bake for 25 to 30 minutes longer, or until the apples are very tender and the glaze has caramelized on the top and around the edges of the tart (it should look almost burnt—dark brown, but *not* blackened). Cool for 5 minutes, then divide among 4 serving plates or dishes and serve.

Makes 4 servings

Per serving: 120 calories, trace protein, 27 g carbohydrates (21 g sugar), 2 g fat, 1 g saturated fat, 5 mg cholesterol, 3 g fiber, 20 mg sodium

GRILLED PEACH AND HONEY PISTACHIO TOWER

Chef Cameron Payne of The Biggest Loser Resort at Fitness Ridge, who created this elegant recipe, suggests garnishing it with additional fresh mint leaves, lemon or orange zest, or a few pistachios. If you opt for the pistachios, just be careful not to overdo it. Each tablespoon adds about 63 calories and 4 grams of fat. Because mint leaves and zest have virtually no calories, feel free to use them as desired.

Chef Payne keeps a Microplane zester on hand for easy zesting and simple cleanup. If you don't have one, any zester will do. Just be sure that you never cut into the pith (the white part) of the peel. If you do, you'll get a bitter burst of flavor, not a pleasant punch.

⅓ cup low-fat ricotta

1 tablespoon honey

1½ tablespoons chopped raw pistachios

⅛ teaspoon lemon zest + additional for garnish

⅛ teaspoon orange zest + additional for garnish

⅛ teaspoon finely chopped fresh mint leaves + additional for garnish

1 large ripe peach, cut into 6 slices

16 navel or blood orange segments

In a small mixing bowl, mix the ricotta, honey, ½ tablespoon of the pistachios, the lemon and orange zest, and mint until well combined. Set it aside.

Preheat the grill to medium heat. Grill the peach slices until warmed through, turning once. In the center of a plate, layer a peach slice, then one orange segment, then 1 tablespoon of ricotta filling. Repeat 2 more times so that all 3 peach slices are topped, then do the same with a second plate. Garnish the plates with the remaining orange sections, mint leaves, pistachios, and orange and lemon zest.

Makes 2 servings

Per serving: 186 calories, 7 g protein, 32 g carbohydrates (26 g sugar), 5 g fat, 2 g saturated fat, 10 mg cholesterol, 4 g fiber, 102 mg sodium

For more ways to live *The Biggest Loser* lifestyle, go to biggestloser.com.

HONEY-DRIZZLED PEAR FAN WITH BLUE CHEESE

This makes a beautiful first course to a buffet or an elegant after-dinner dessert to impress friends (it should be eaten with a fork, not your hands, as the pear slices are very thin). In fact, it's very much in line with "what the French would do"—a far cry from diet food. If you're in a hurry, just chop the pears and throw everything together in a to-go container for a quick snack.

½ medium pear (any variety), cored and very thinly sliced lengthwise

½ ounce crumbled reduced-fat blue cheese (about 2 tablespoons)

½ teaspoon honey

Arrange the pear slices on an appetizer plate so the slices are touching in the center and point outward (they can overlap slightly), creating a circular "fan" pattern. Sprinkle the blue cheese evenly over the pears. Drizzle the honey evenly over top. Serve immediately.

Makes 1 serving

Per serving: 101 calories, 4 g protein, 16 g carbohydrates (11 g sugar), 3 g fat, 2 g saturated fat, 8 mg cholesterol, 2 g fiber, 192 mg sodium

Biggest Loser Trainer Tip: Jillian Michaels

You owe the world one thing and that is to be uniquely yourself and to take care of yourself. That's the best gift that you could give anyone—to make sure that your heart and your head are together.

MERINGUE-TOPPED PINK GRAPEFRUIT

This delicious combination of sweet and sour can be made with any variety of grapefruit. I particularly love the pretty pink color peeking from the cloud of meringue. If the grapefruit halves seem wobbly as you place them on the baking dish, slice off a very thin portion from the bottom (not the cut side) so they sit flat—just be sure to make the cut thin enough that you're only cutting peel, not into the fruit.

2 medium pink grapefruit

2 cups "Cut the Crap" Whipped Topping (page 217)

Preheat the oven to 350°F. Line a medium baking sheet with parchment paper.

Cut both grapefruit in half crosswise and remove any visible seeds. Using a grapefruit knife or small paring knife, cut in between the membranes of each half (this will make the flesh easier to eat once it's topped). Set the grapefruit halves on the prepared baking sheet. Top each half evenly with the whipped topping (about ½ cup on each).

Bake for 20 to 25 minutes, or until the topping is golden brown on top and the grapefruit is warmed through.

Makes 4 servings

Per serving: 89 calories, 1 g protein, 22 g carbohydrates (21 g sugar), trace fat, trace saturated fat, 0 mg cholesterol, 1 g fiber, 10 mg sodium

BEIN' BOLD BALSAMIC BERRIES

I love serving these berries in a martini glass to give them an elegant air. Feel free to add fresh mint or fresh basil to the top just before serving for a kick of calorie-free flavor. I recommend using an aged vinegar for this recipe, if possible—they tend to be better quality and will give this sweet, simple ending a richer taste.

---

1 tablespoon balsamic vinegar

2 teaspoons honey

1 cup quartered strawberries

Add the vinegar and honey to a medium resealable glass or plastic container. With a mini-whisk, whisk until well combined. Add the strawberries and toss until they're well coated. Cover and refrigerate for 30 minutes.

Toss the berries again and transfer them to a martini glass (or other small serving bowl). Serve immediately.

Makes 1 serving

Per serving: 106 calories, 1 g protein, 26 g carbohydrates (21 g sugar), <1 g fat, trace saturated fat, 0 mg cholesterol, 3 g fiber, 7 mg sodium

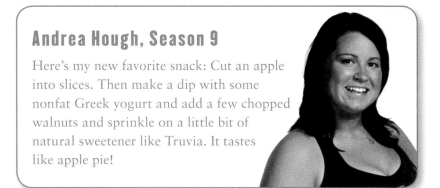

Andrea Hough, Season 9

Here's my new favorite snack: Cut an apple into slices. Then make a dip with some nonfat Greek yogurt and add a few chopped walnuts and sprinkle on a little bit of natural sweetener like Truvia. It tastes like apple pie!

STRAWBERRY DAIQUIRI CREAM PIE

Make sure you refrigerate this pie for the full 12 hours, as indicated, to ensure it sets completely and will easily slice into wedges. Because it has to sit overnight, this is a great dessert to make ahead of time for guests. One slice contains just 126 calories, so if you'd like to make it a little more indulgent, feel free to use whole wheat graham crackers for the crust instead of the cereal. Just keep in mind that even most natural whole wheat graham crackers contain cane sugar.

Butter-flavored cooking spray

¾ cup whole grain, crunchy, high-fiber, low-sugar cereal (I used Kashi 7 Whole Grain Nuggets)

2 tablespoons 100% fruit strawberry spread

1¼ cups fat-free, fruit juice–sweetened vanilla yogurt (I used Cascade Fresh)

⅓ cup cold water

3 tablespoons freshly squeezed lime juice

1 packet (.25 ounce) unflavored gelatin

2½ cups trimmed fresh strawberries

3 tablespoons light agave nectar

2 tablespoons dark or light rum

¼ teaspoon salt

4 strawberries cut in half lengthwise

"Cut the Crap" Whipped Topping (page 217), optional

Preheat the oven to 350°F. Lightly mist a 9"-diameter pie plate with cooking spray.

Add the cereal to the bowl of a food processor fitted with a chopping blade. Process for 15 to 20 seconds, or until the cereal is crushed. Transfer the cereal to a small mixing bowl and add the fruit spread. Mix until well combined (the mixture should be slightly sticky). Pour the cereal mixture into the prepared pie plate. Using a small piece of parchment paper, gently press the cereal mixture evenly across the bottom and up the sides of the pie plate. Bake for 7 to 9 minutes, or until lightly golden brown. Allow it to cool completely.

Meanwhile, spoon the yogurt into a clean, lint-free cotton dish towel. Carefully pull together all corners of the towel to create a pouch around the yogurt (be sure to grab all sides of the towel or the yogurt will leak out). Gently twist the towel one or two times, or until a steady stream of liquid starts to drip from it (do not twist too much or the yogurt will squish out of the towel). Allow the yogurt to strain until a steady stream of liquid no longer runs from the towel (a few drops of liquid are okay). Place the towel-wrapped yogurt in a strainer over a bowl. Set it aside.

(continued)

In a small saucepan, mix the water and lime juice. Sprinkle the gelatin over the top. Set it aside.

In a food processor fitted with a chopping blade, puree the strawberries until smooth, pausing to scrape down the sides of the bowl with a rubber spatula, if necessary. Transfer them to a medium mixing bowl. Stir in the agave, rum, and salt. Set the mixture aside.

Place the gelatin mixture over low heat. Using a wooden spoon, stir the mixture constantly until the gelatin is completely dissolved. Pour it into the strawberry mixture.

Using a rubber spatula, scrape the strained yogurt from the towel and add it to the strawberry mixture. Using a sturdy whisk, stir until well combined. Pour the filling into the prepared crust. Place a dinner plate upside down over the pie dish to cover it. Refrigerate the pie on a level shelf overnight (at least 12 hours), or until it is completely set. Arrange the strawberry slices, cut sides down, around the outer edges of the pie to garnish. Slice into 8 equal wedges and top with a dollop of whipped topping, if desired. Serve immediately, or cover and refrigerate for up to 3 days.

Makes 8 servings

Per serving: 126 calories, 4 g protein, 26 g carbohydrates (15 g sugar), trace fat, trace saturated fat, 0 mg cholesterol, 2 g fiber, 143 mg sodium

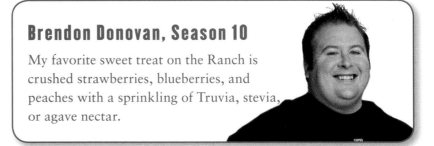

Brendon Donovan, Season 10

My favorite sweet treat on the Ranch is crushed strawberries, blueberries, and peaches with a sprinkling of Truvia, stevia, or agave nectar.

SWEET & SOUR POWER GRAPES

I prefer my sweet snacks of this type to be on the smaller side—sometimes I just need something sweet to take the edge off a craving. But you can easily double this recipe for a larger snack that's still less than 150 calories.

1 tablespoon low-fat sour cream

1½ teaspoons coconut sugar

10 large seedless grapes (any variety)

Spoon the sour cream and sugar into separate, small bowls. Dip each grape first into the sour cream, then the sugar, and eat!

Makes 1 serving

Per serving: 74 calories, < 1 g protein, 17 g carbohydrates (13 g sugar), 1 g fat, < 1 g saturated fat, 5 mg cholesterol, trace fiber, 29 mg sodium

Sean Algaier, Season 8

Look at me. It is possible to lose weight and get healthy plus have a family and a job and a real life. Anybody in the world can do it. Just sit down, make a plan, and stick to it. Don't go blindly into it. Map out some baby steps.

BIGGEST

CREAMY NO-CONSEQUENCE FRUIT SALAD

Though this recipe is far from a traditional ambrosia, the creamy texture and coconut make it reminiscent of one. Fortunately, the sugars consumed here won't spike your blood sugar.

Make sure to use a firm banana when preparing this fruit salad to achieve an ideal consistency. You want the creaminess of the dressing to contrast with the fresh, firm fruit pieces.

---

1 cup trimmed, quartered strawberries

1 cup bite-size apple chunks (any variety)

¼ cup fat-free, fruit juice–sweetened vanilla yogurt

2 tablespoons finely shredded reduced-fat unsweetened coconut (I used Let's Do . . . Organic 40% less fat coconut)

1 cup ½"-thick banana slices

Add the strawberries, apples, yogurt, and coconut to a medium resealable plastic container and stir until well combined. Add the bananas and stir gently until just combined. Refrigerate for at least 2 hours. Divide between 2 serving bowls and serve or keep refrigerated for up to 2 days.

Makes 2 servings

Per serving: 182 calories, 3 g protein, 37 g carbohydrates (23 g sugar), 4 g fat, 3 g saturated fat, 0 mg cholesterol, 6 g fiber, 17 mg sodium

Julio Gomez, Season 8

Let go of the fear and just go with it. Know that you can do this and move forward. And make yourself accountable for not only getting to the gym but for putting forth a real effort once you're there.

PEACH BLACKBERRY BETTY

Fruit betties and crumbles are usually extremely calorie dense—even worse than chocolate cake in many cases—because they contain so much sugar and butter and because the fruit shrinks substantially during the cooking process. Here I used blackberries with peaches because in addition to being a great flavor combination, the blackberries shrink less than many other fruits.

I usually like to cut the peaches in half, then peel them, as opposed to doing it the other way around. I find that I waste less fruit if I halve them before cutting them.

Butter-flavored cooking spray

¼ cup whole grain oat flour

3 cups 1" cubes peeled firm peaches (about 3 medium peaches)

3 cups fresh blackberries

¼ cup + 2 tablespoons light agave nectar

2 tablespoons freshly squeezed lemon juice

¾ cup old-fashioned oats

2 tablespoons very cold unsalted butter, cut into cubes

1 tablespoon 100% fruit blackberry spread

Preheat the oven to 350°F. Lightly mist an 8" × 8" glass or ceramic baking dish with cooking spray.

Add the flour to the bowl of a mini-food processor fitted with a chopping blade. Process it for 2 minutes.

In a medium mixing bowl, mix the peaches, blackberries, agave, lemon juice, and flour until well combined. Transfer the mixture to the prepared baking dish. Set aside.

In a small mixing bowl, combine the oats, butter, and fruit spread using a pastry blender until well combined. Sprinkle the oat mixture evenly over the top of the fruit mixture. Bake for 45 to 50 minutes, or until the fruit is tender and hot throughout and the topping is golden brown (only some juices should remain in the bottom of the pan; it shouldn't be runny). Transfer the dish to a wire rack and cool for about 5 minutes. Cut into 6 pieces. Serve immediately.

Makes 6 servings

Per serving: 215 calories, 4 g protein, 41 g carbohydrates (27 g sugar), 5 g fat, 2 g saturated fat, 10 mg cholesterol, 6 g fiber, 1 mg sodium

MANGO FLOWER ON A STICK

It can be challenging to convince children to choose fruit for snack time or dessert. But with a little TLC, you can create something really special that they'll get excited about. This mango flower is a perfect example. By putting it on a stick and cutting it into "petals," they're more likely to grab a fresh mango than dig through the cookie jar.

For the grown-ups in your home, you can add a punch of flavor by squeezing fresh lime juice on top and sprinkling on a little cayenne pepper.

1 ripe medium mango, peeled

You will need a 4"-to-6"-long metal skewer with a sharp point at one end.

Hold the mango vertically upright on your cutting board so the more narrow end points upward. Picture the petals of a rose, then carefully, using a sharp knife, cut a thin slice starting from the top of the mango, working your way down to the base, without cutting all the way through the fruit (you are creating the outside layer of "petals"). Fold the "petal" down, then rotate the mango about 30 degrees. Repeat the process, gently bending the "petals" outward away from the pit, but being careful not to break the fruit, until you get to the pit in the center and can no longer slice the fruit. Carefully press the flower petals back toward the center to briefly return the fruit to its original shape.

Turn the fruit upside down and insert the skewer into the pit until you can't push it any further. Using a meat mallet, hammer the skewer firmly into the fruit. Hold the stick upright (like a lollipop) and reopen the petals so it looks like a flower. Serve immediately.

Makes 1 serving

Per serving: 135 calories, 1 g protein, 35 g carbohydrates (31 g sugar), <1 g fat, trace saturated fat, 0 mg cholesterol, 4 g fiber, 4 mg sodium

STRAWBERRY CLOUD SOUFFLÉS

This dessert is extremely light both in consistency and in consequence. It's ideal to serve the soufflés immediately—as they cool, they do deflate—but truth be told, they're delish out of the refrigerator the next day. They're not nearly as pretty by then, but they actually taste a bit sweeter. Heck, for less than 75 calories, you can have one at night and one from the refrigerator the next day!

Butter-flavored cooking spray

- ½ cup chopped fresh strawberries
- ¼ cup coconut sugar
- 1 tablespoon coconut rum
- 3 large egg whites
- ⅛ teaspoon cream of tartar

Preheat the oven to 375°F. Lightly mist four 3½"-diameter (½-cup capacity) ramekins with cooking spray.

In the bowl of a blender or a mini-food processor fitted with a chopping blade, process the strawberries, pausing to scrape down the sides of the bowl if necessary, until they are completely smooth. Place a fine mesh strainer over a medium mixing bowl. Pour the strawberry puree into the strainer and using a spatula, press it through the strainer. Stir in the sugar and rum until well combined. Set aside.

Add the egg whites and cream of tartar to a clean, dry, medium glass or metal mixing bowl. Using a hand or stand mixer fitted with the whisk attachment, beat the whites until they are stiff but not dry. Using a spatula, gently fold the whites in 3 additions into the strawberry puree, being careful not to overmix. Divide the mixture evenly among the prepared ramekins.

Bake for 10 to 12 minutes, or until the soufflés have poofed well above the dish and are golden brown on top and are no longer runny inside when poked in the center with a butter knife. Serve immediately.

Makes 4 soufflés

Per soufflé: 73 calories, 3 g protein, 15 g carbohydrates (10 g sugar), trace fat, trace saturated fat, 0 mg cholesterol, <1 g fiber, 70 mg sodium

KIWI MANGO PINEAPPLE CREPES

I was lucky enough to visit The Biggest Loser Resort at Fitness Ridge this year, which was an incredible experience. Who would've thought 7 hours (per day!) of working out could feel self-indulgent? We went on beautiful hikes, and each person I met had such wonderful energy that it was a pleasure to be there. But the best part was getting to eat Chef Cameron Payne's scrumptious creations. This crepe recipe, which he kindly agreed to share with us, is a great reflection of The Biggest Loser *lifestyle and his delicious and healthy cuisine.*

For the crepe:

⅓ cup whole grain oat flour

6 egg whites

⅔ cup unsweetened rice milk

2 tablespoons soy nut butter

¼ teaspoon sea salt

Butter-flavored cooking spray

For the crepe filling:

2 cups all-natural low-fat ricotta cheese

¼ cup + 1 tablespoon honey

1 teaspoon lemon zest

1 cup ½" mango cubes

½ cup ½" kiwi cubes

½ cup ½" pineapple cubes

For the tropical topping:

½ cup ½" kiwi cubes

½ cup ½" mango cubes

½ cup ½" pineapple cubes

To prepare the crepes: Sift the flour into a medium mixing bowl. In a second medium mixing bowl, using a sturdy whisk, mix the egg whites, milk, soy nut butter, and salt until well incorporated. Slowly pour the mixture into the bowl with the flour and mix just until no lumps remain, being sure not to overmix. Cover and refrigerate it for 1 hour.

To prepare the filling: In a small mixing bowl, stir the ricotta, honey, and lemon zest until mixed thoroughly. Add the mango, kiwi, and pineapple and very carefully fold them into the ricotta mixture. Cover and refrigerate until ready to use.

To prepare the topping: In a small mixing bowl, stir the kiwi, mango, and pineapple until well combined. Cover and refrigerate until ready to use.

 For more ways to live *The Biggest Loser* lifestyle, go to biggestloser.com.

To make and assemble the crepes: Place a nonstick crepe pan or nonstick griddle over medium heat. Lightly mist it with cooking spray. When hot, ladle 3 tablespoons of the batter into the pan. Tilt the pan with a circular motion to create a circle of batter that is about 5½" in diameter. Cook for 30 seconds to 1 minute, or until lightly golden on the bottom and set enough to flip. Using a large spatula, carefully flip it. Cook the crepe for 30 seconds to 1 minute longer, or until it is cooked through and a light golden brown. Transfer it to a plate or large, clean, flat work surface to cool. Repeat the process 7 times to create 8 crepes. (Once they are cool, you can layer them with parchment paper, if desired).

Place one crepe flat on a plate or on your work surface. Add a scant ½ cup of the filling and roll the crepe, enchilada-style. Spread ¼ cup of the topping evenly over the top. Repeat with the remaining crepes.

Makes 8 servings

Per serving: 198 calories, 12 g protein, 30 g carbohydrates (22 g sugar), 5 g fat, 2 g saturated fat, 20 mg cholesterol, 2 g fiber, 266 mg sodium

Danny Cahill, Season 8 Winner

When you eat healthy foods for a while, your taste buds begin to appreciate the sweetness of a simple piece of fruit. But if you go out to dinner and really want to order something more decadent—order a smaller size dessert and split it with a friend. You can satisfy your craving with just a couple bites.

BLACK TEAM BANANA BOAT

This dessert is super simple and just might take you back to childhood if you ever roasted bananas over a campfire. Note that the banana peel will turn black in the oven. Don't worry, you're not burning it!

1 medium banana (about 7"), unpeeled

1 tablespoon Chocolate "Fudge" Sauce (page 215)

1 teaspoon finely shredded unsweetened reduced-fat coconut (I used Let's Do . . . Organic)

Preheat the oven to 350°F.

Hold the banana with the ends facing up. Slice lengthwise down the center of the banana, about ½" from one end to ½" from the other, creating a pocket (make sure not to slice all the way through). Place the banana on a small baking sheet, cut side up. Push the ends toward each other to "open" the banana until it stands upright.

Spoon the fudge sauce evenly in the center of the banana. Sprinkle the coconut over the fudge.

Bake for 10 to 12 minutes, or until soft. Using a fork, mash the cooked banana, sauce, and coconut together. Eat it straight from the peel or scoop it into a bowl and serve immediately.

Makes 1 serving

Per serving: **161 calories, 2 g protein, 41 g carbohydrates (32 g sugar), <1 g fat, <1 g saturated fat, 0 mg cholesterol, 5 g fiber, trace sodium**

Koli Palu, Season 9

You really have to plan your meals and prepare them beforehand. The less prepared you are, the more likely you are to grab something from the vending machine.

4

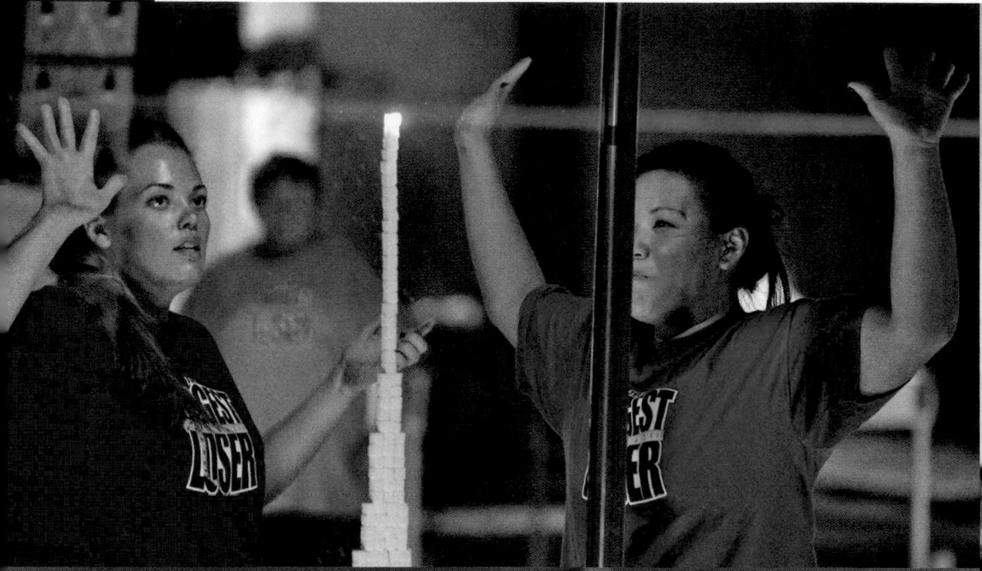

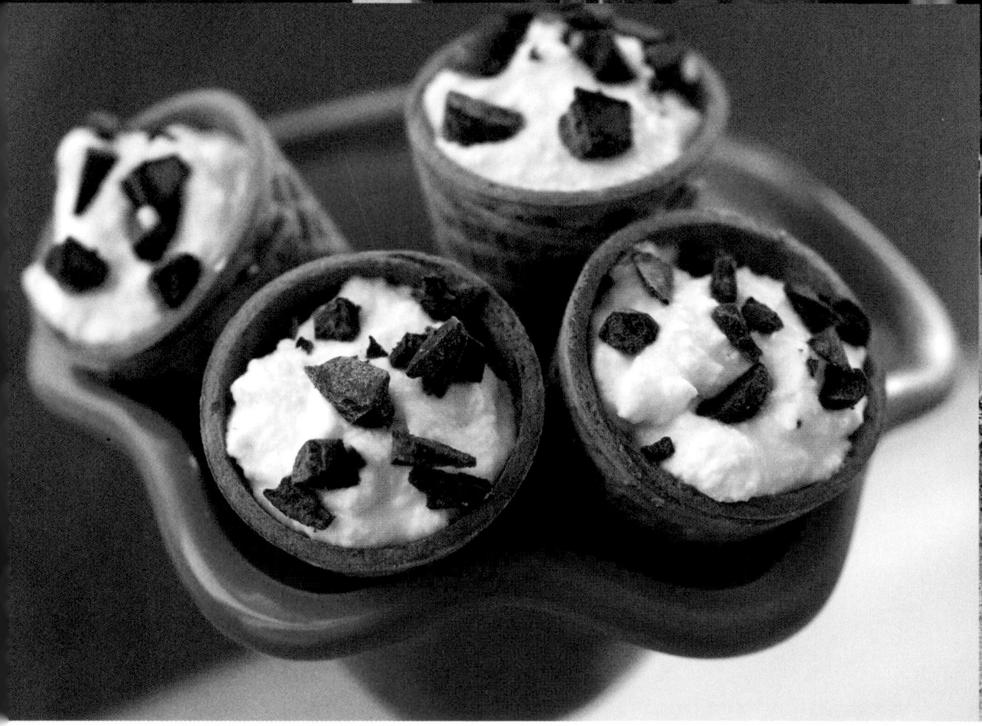

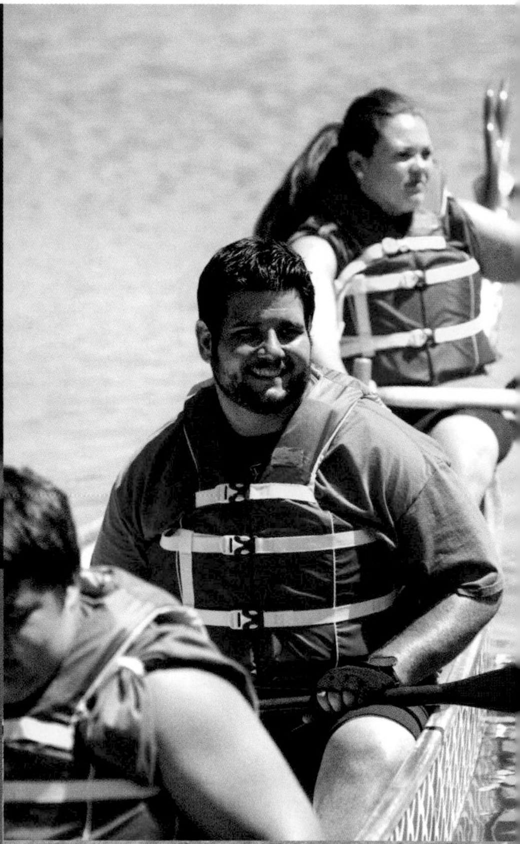

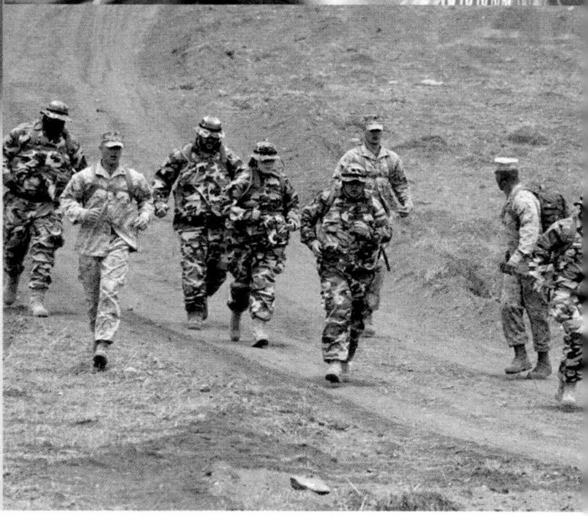

Sweet Snacks

When it comes to whipping up healthy snacks to satisfy their sweet tooth, *The Biggest Loser* contestants get very creative. Fortunately, with a well-stocked kitchen at the Ranch, they can't get themselves into too much trouble.

The contestants who have young kids at home are especially interested in learning how to create healthier versions of snack-time favorites, and they're eager to pass on what they've learned about nutrition to their kids. Dina Mercado of Season 8 says that when it comes to snack time, she gives her young son choices. "Since he's a kid, I always give him the option of the healthy snack or the not-so-healthy snack. But I tell him what each choice is going to do for his body, she says. "He still sometimes goes for the not-so-healthy choice, but more and more he picks the healthy snack."

BiggestLoserClub.com nutrition expert Greg Hottinger, RD, says it's important to consider the quality of the calories as well as the portion size when choosing snack foods. "Eating fat-free or low-fat snacks doesn't always deliver what you're looking for," says Hottinger. "There's always room in your diet for having a taste of the real thing, in moderation."

Season 8 winner Danny Cahill says one of the joys of going back home was teaching his kids about how to make healthy choices. "It's *so* much better than what I was teaching them before," he says. "I went to my children's school and brought bags of potato chips and air-popped popcorn. I showed them how they could eat a lot more popcorn for the same amount of calories as just a few chips and with much less fat. It helps kids to see the difference in quantity in order to understand nutrition. It's okay for them to eat a potato chip now and again, as long as they don't do it all of the time."

The beauty of all the snack recipes in this chapter is how quickly and painlessly you can stock your family's kitchen with healthy, on-the-go treats that satisfy without a lot of calories. In fact, there's one sweet snack in this chapter (Sparkling Black Cherry Squares, page 87) that contains just 25 calories per serving! Chef Devin says, "It's not the most indulgent recipe, but at the end of the night when you want a little something sweet, it hits the spot."

10 Snacks for a Sweet Tooth

BiggestLoserClub.com nutrition expert Greg Hottinger, RD, shares these quick snack ideas that offer a lot of sweet satisfaction for 150 calories or less.

1. 2 Fig Newtons (110 calories)
2. ½ cup Total cereal with ½ cup nonfat milk and 10 raspberries (125 calories)
3. ½ cup sliced strawberries with ½ cup nonfat plain yogurt (100 calories)
4. Frozen fruit bar (110 calories—check label)
5. Baked apple: Core a medium apple; mix ¼ cup cooked brown rice with cinnamon and 1 tablespoon raisins and stuff into the center of the apple. Bake at 350°F until tender (150 calories).
6. Lindt chocolate ball (70 calories)
7. Fudgsicle (100 calories)
8. ½ cup sorbet made with real fruit (look for brands with 100 calories per ½ cup)
9. Whaguru Chew (150 calories—available at natural food stores)
10. ½ cup pudding, low-fat (100 calories)

"NEW"-TELLA PIZZA

I love the taste of Nutella—the delicious combination of hazelnuts and chocolate just shouldn't be avoided. So here I've created a natural ("new") alternative that tastes just as great and allows you (and me!) to indulge more often.

1 reduced-fat whole wheat flour tortilla (7" diameter) (see note)

½ tablespoon creamy unsalted unsweetened hazelnut butter

2 teaspoons Chocolate "Fudge" Sauce (page 215)

Preheat the oven to 400°F.

Place the tortilla on a small, nonstick baking sheet. Bake for 3 to 4 minutes per side, watching carefully, or until completely crisp through. If air bubbles form during baking, open the oven, poke the bubbles with a fork, then use a spatula or oven mitt to press the air out. Transfer the tortilla to a serving plate. Spread the hazelnut butter evenly over the tortilla, leaving about a ½" border. Drizzle the fudge sauce evenly over the pizza. Slice into 4 or 8 wedges and serve immediately.

Note: I don't recommend using a low-carb tortilla in this recipe. Look for a whole grain or whole wheat option that is low in fat and about 110 calories. The low-carb ones won't crisp properly in the oven and won't taste right either.

Makes 1 serving

Per serving: **185** calories, **5** g protein, **32** g carbohydrates (**7** g sugar), **6** g fat, trace saturated fat, **0** mg cholesterol, **4** g fiber, **135** mg sodium

Biggest Loser Trainer Tip: Jillian Michaels

Happiness comes with the achievement of little goals. With little tiny steps that you take every single day, you'll have a little accomplishment that will teach you a different reality. You have everything that it takes to achieve anything that you want. It will not be easy. But it will be worth it.

RASPBERRY "JELLY ROLLS"

I included a recipe for Better Blueberry Pancakes in the first Biggest Loser Cookbook that I continually receive fan letters about. Since they've been so well received, I've created these not-exactly-jelly-rolls using that pancake batter as a base instead of buttery, sugary cake batter. These pickup-able sweet treats are perfect for kids and grown-ups alike. And if you love them as much as I do, you can keep the batter prepared in your refrigerator for a few days so it's ready when a craving hits!

½ cup low-fat buttermilk

½ cup whole grain oat flour

1 large egg white, lightly beaten

½ teaspoon baking soda

¼ teaspoon vanilla extract

¼ teaspoon salt

1 tablespoon water

Butter-flavored cooking spray

2 tablespoons + 2 teaspoons 100% fruit raspberry spread

⅛ teaspoon unsweetened cocoa powder (optional)

In a small bowl, combine the buttermilk, flour, egg white, baking soda, vanilla, salt, and water. Whisk until just blended. Let stand for 10 minutes.

Heat a large, nonstick skillet over medium heat until it is hot enough for a spritz of water to sizzle on it. With an oven mitt, briefly remove the pan from the heat to mist lightly with cooking spray. Return the pan to the heat. Pour two ¼-cup dollops of batter onto the skillet (half of the batter should remain). Cook for 2 minutes, or until bubbles appear on the tops and the bottoms are golden brown. Flip. Cook for 2 minutes, or until browned on the bottom. Transfer the finished "cakes" to a cutting board or flat work surface. Re-spray the pan and cook the remaining batter to make 4 total.

Place the finished "cakes," with the sides that were cooked first, facedown on your work surface. Spread each evenly with 2 teaspoons of the fruit spread, leaving about ½" of one edge bare. Gently roll each "cake" from the filled edge to the bare edge into a tube shape, being careful that the spread does not gush out. Arrange them on a serving plate, seam sides down. Transfer the cocoa powder, if desired, to a fine sieve or sifter and lightly dust the tops of the rolls evenly with the cocoa. Serve immediately.

Makes 4 servings

Per serving: 84 calories, 4 g protein, 14 g carbohydrates (7 g sugar), 1 g fat, trace saturated fat, 2 mg cholesterol, 1 g fiber, 351 mg sodium

CONE-NOLIS

If you have any trouble finding dark chocolate chunks, which are most commonly sold at natural food stores, you can buy any dark chocolate (dark chocolate is rich in antioxidants and thus the best choice) and chop it into ¼" (or smaller) pieces for this recipe. When you open the container of ricotta, be sure to drain any liquid that may be sitting on the top. It'll make for a much creamier, richer filling.

---

1 cup all-natural low-fat ricotta cheese

1 tablespoon amaretto-flavored agave nectar

1 tablespoon natural 70% cocoa mini dark chocolate chunks, coarsely chopped

4 naturally sweetened wheat sugar cones (I used Let's Do . . . Organic)

Using a whisk, mix the ricotta, agave, and ½ tablespoon of the chocolate until combined. Cover the mixture and refrigerate for at least 1 hour to allow the filling to chill and the flavors to meld.

Divide the ricotta mixture evenly among the four cones (about ¼ cup each). Sprinkle the remaining chocolate pieces evenly over the cones. Serve immediately.

Makes 4 servings

Per serving: 143 calories, 7 g protein, 18 g carbohydrates (7 g sugar), 4 g fat, 3 g saturated fat, 20 mg cholesterol, <1 g fiber, 160 mg sodium

Suzanne Mendonca, Season 2

When I want a sweet snack, I like to spread a graham cracker square with fat-free cream cheese. I usually put fruit spread or fresh berries on top of it.

MIXED BERRY DESSERT NACHOS

This recipe is a sweet spin on traditional nachos that is just as fun and just as messy as the savory version. And the whole grain "chips" and fruit offer a nice boost of belly-filling fiber.

1   reduced-fat whole wheat flour tortilla (7" diameter) (see note)

1   tablespoon egg substitute

½   teaspoon coconut sugar

⅓   cup blueberries

⅓   cup stemmed and chopped strawberries

2   tablespoons Raspberry Tapenade (page 216)

Preheat the oven to 400°F. Line a small baking sheet with parchment paper.

Lightly brush the tortilla evenly with half of the egg substitute and sprinkle ¼ teaspoon of the sugar over top. Flip over and repeat on the other side. Cut the tortilla into 8 equal wedges. Transfer the wedges to the prepared baking sheet, so they do not touch. Bake for 2 to 4 minutes per side, or until they are completely crisp and lightly browned. Allow them to cool completely, about 10 minutes.

Arrange the cooled chips in a medium shallow bowl. Top them with the blueberries, followed by the strawberries. Drizzle the Raspberry Tapenade over top and serve immediately.

Note: I don't recommend using a low-carb tortilla in this recipe. Look for a whole grain or whole wheat option that is low in fat and about 110 calories. The low-carb ones won't crisp properly in the oven and won't taste right either.

Makes 1 serving

Per serving: 183 calories, 5 g protein, 41 g carbohydrates (9 g sugar), 3 g fat, trace saturated fat, 0 mg cholesterol, 6 g fiber, 155 mg sodium

Biggest Loser Trainer Tip: Bob Harper

A lot of people harbor the false notion that skipping a meal during the day will help them shed pounds. However, this inevitably leads to massive bingeing at night. Instead, eat your bigger meals earlier in the day and progressively downsize the later it gets.

MOCHA SILK CUSTARD

This is a delicious treat to have on hand for coffee and chocolate lovers. It has a fraction of the fat and calories of mocha coffee drinks or chocolate custards, and it's simple to put together.

To make this dessert extra special, I sometimes top it with crushed chocolate-covered espresso beans and a little whipped topping. To crush the espresso beans, just place them in a resealable plastic bag and give them a few pounds with a meat mallet. Three espresso beans per dessert add about 20 calories and 1 gram of fat (and 1 tablespoon of "Cut the Crap" Whipped Topping will add about 8 calories).

---

1 large omega-3 egg

1 tablespoon unsweetened chocolate almond milk

1 packet (0.25 ounce) unflavored gelatin

½ tablespoon instant espresso powder

1 cup boiling water

½ cup cold fat-free evaporated milk

½ cup all-natural low-fat ricotta cheese

⅓ cup coconut sugar

3 tablespoons unsweetened cocoa powder

18 dark chocolate–covered, naturally sweetened espresso beans, crushed (optional)

6 tablespoons "Cut the Crap" Whipped Topping (page 217), optional

In a blender, combine the egg, almond milk, gelatin, and espresso powder. Blend on high speed for 15 seconds. Using a rubber spatula, scrape down the sides of the blender, then blend the ingredients for another 10 seconds. Let the mixture stand for 1 minute, then add the boiling water and immediately blend for another 15 seconds, or until the gelatin is dissolved. Add the evaporated milk, ricotta, sugar, and cocoa and blend for 1 minute longer, or until the mixture is smooth.

Divide the mixture evenly among six 3½" (approximately ½-cup capacity) ramekins or decorative custard dishes. Cover each with plastic wrap and refrigerate for at least 3 hours, or until set. Top with espresso beans and whipped topping, if desired, just before serving.

Makes 6 servings

Per serving: 104 calories, 6 g protein, 16 g carbohydrates (11 g sugar), 2 g fat, <1 g saturated fat, 42 mg cholesterol, <1 g fiber, 117 mg sodium

APPLE CINNAMON ON-THE-RIGHT-TRAIL MIX

Trail mix commonly contains dried fruit, which is great because it's all natural. However, dried fruit can be very calorie dense. Here I've used baked-dried fruit (sometimes referred to as freeze-dried), which has become very popular in recent years. A whole cup of the baked-dried apples has 116 calories. A cup of most traditionally dried apples has about 220 calories.

For portion control, it might be best to portion the trail mix as soon as you make it. Though this version is much lower in calories and fat than most you'll find, it's so yummy that it's still easy to over-indulge.

---

1 cup fruit juice– or molasses-sweetened whole oat or whole grain cinnamon cereal (I used Barbara's Bakery Cinnamon Crunch Shredded Oats Cereal)

1 cup baked-dried cinnamon apple chips

¼ cup raisins

⅛ cup reduced-salt, dry roasted almonds

Mix the cereal, apple chips, raisins, and almonds in a resealable plastic container until combined. Serve immediately or scoop by ½ cupfuls into snack-size resealable plastic bags for on-the-go snacking.

Makes 5 (½-cup) servings

Per serving: 113 calories, 2 g protein, 22 g carbohydrates (15 g sugar), 2 g fat, trace saturated fat, 0 mg cholesterol, 2 g fiber, 66 mg sodium

Vicky Andrews, Season 9

Losing weight offers you an opportunity to do great things. Think of yourself as an inspiration to others, and they'll pay it forward just as you're doing. Work as hard on your weight loss as possible!

CHOCOLATE-GLAZED SOFT PRETZEL BITES

Adding a sprinkle of sea salt to chocolate has emerged as a trend in recent years. And it doesn't surprise me—it's such a delicious way to satisfy sweet and salty cravings at once.

Whole wheat pizza dough provides a great base for these everyone-friendly bites topped with a mouthwatering glaze. Though it might be tempting to make extra pretzels in order to have leftovers, pretzels are really best eaten the same day, so be sure not to overdo it!

---

2 tablespoons baking soda

8 ounces whole wheat pizza dough (no more than 3 grams of fat per 2-ounce serving), fresh or frozen and defrosted

1 tablespoon + 1 teaspoon Chocolate "Fudge" Sauce (page 215)

Sea salt, to taste

Preheat the oven to 450°F. Line a large baking sheet with parchment paper.

Add enough water to a large soup pot so it's one-quarter full. Add the baking soda. Place the pot over high heat and bring the water to a boil.

Using a sharp knife or pastry cutter, cut the dough into 2 equal portions. Remove one of the portions to a cutting board. Roll the dough into a 20"-long rope. Cut the rope into 8 equal pieces. Repeat the process with the remaining dough, leaving you with 16 dough pieces.

Add the pieces to the water in a single layer, working in batches if necessary, and boil them for 1 to 2 minutes, or until they float. Using a slotted spoon to drain off any excess water, remove the boiled dough pieces to the prepared baking sheet in a single layer, so they do not touch.

Bake the pretzels for 10 to 12 minutes, or until lightly browned. Let them cool for 2 to 3 minutes, then spread ¼ teaspoon fudge sauce over the top of each pretzel bite. Sprinkle each with a few crystals of salt, or to taste. Arrange them on a serving platter and serve immediately.

Makes 16

Per serving (4 pretzels): 144 calories, 4 g protein, 28 g carbohydrates (4 g sugar), 2 g fat, trace saturated fat, 0 mg cholesterol, 3 g fiber, 127 sodium

BERRY SKEWERS 'N DIP

Skewering berries and serving them with dip just plain makes them more appealing. If you're anything like me, I love berries, but they're not always the first thing I reach for in my refrigerator. But when they're skewered and sitting on the table for children or guests, they get gobbled up at record speed, especially when accompanied by this great cream-cheesy dip. This filling snack offers a nice serving of fruit, so you can feel good about eating it or serving it to your family.

---

12 medium strawberries, trimmed

27 blueberries

2 tablespoons Vanilla Cream Cheese Dip (page 219)

You'll need three 8" or 12" skewers. Thread a strawberry, followed by 3 blueberries, onto one of the skewers. Continue skewering the fruit in this fashion (skewer the strawberries so they are facing the same direction), until you have 4 strawberries and 9 blueberries on a skewer. Repeat with the remaining berries and skewers.

Place the skewers on a serving plate. Spoon the dip into a small bowl and serve it alongside the skewers for dipping. Serve immediately.

Makes 1 serving

Per serving: 187 calories, 4 g protein, 29 g carbohydrates (23 g sugar), 6 g fat, 4 g saturated fat, 20 mg cholesterol, 4 g fiber, 140 mg sodium

Elizabeth Ruiz, Season 10

I add a little vanilla extract and Truvia to Greek yogurt. It reminds me of flan, which is my favorite sweet treat.

PEACHES & CREAM

I love to make this quick and easy dessert, particularly in the late summer months when peaches are at their most delicious. Though fresh should be your first choice, you can always use frozen peaches in the off-season. Believe it or not, a traditional peaches and cream parfait very similar to this one can have as many as 600 calories and 35 grams of fat!

If you're serving this to guests and want to ensure a pretty presentation, freeze the whipped topping for a few hours before serving, then spoon it into a pastry bag to do the layering. Your dessert will be picture-perfect.

---

1 **firm small peach, halved, peeled, and pitted**

⅓ **cup "Cut the Crap" Whipped Topping (page 217)**

Cut the peach halves into ½"-thick slices. Cut each slice in half crosswise. Place half of the peach slices in the bottom of a wine or parfait glass. Top them with half of the whipped topping, spreading it evenly over the peaches. Top with the remaining peaches, followed by the remaining whipped topping. Serve immediately or cover tightly with plastic wrap and refrigerate for up to 1 day.

Makes 1 serving

Per serving: 83 calories, 2 g protein, 20 g carbohydrates (19 g sugar), trace fat, trace saturated fat, 0 mg cholesterol, 2 g fiber, 7 mg sodium

Koli Palu, Season 9

There will be times you have setbacks and plateaus. But it's about staying in motion, not giving up. There may be times you miss a day working out, but just get up and do it the next day. The mental and emotional part of this journey is just as important as the physical part.

SPARKLING BLACK CHERRY SQUARES

This sweet treat is a staple for me—it's less than 30 calories per serving and is a great go-to recipe for when cravings strike. Not only is it low in calories, but since it's made with gelatin, it also contains protein. I love using Steaz Black Cherry Sparkling Green Tea because it makes such pretty blocks, especially around the holiday season, but it does have a mild flavor. If you prefer a bolder punch, try making this with your favorite zero-calorie stevia-sweetened soda.

When measuring the soda, make sure not to measure the bubbly fizz, just the soda.

---

4 cups Steaz Zero Calorie Black Cherry Sparkling Green Tea, or other zero-calorie stevia-sweetened soda

4 packets (0.25 ounce each) unflavored gelatin

4 fresh cherries (optional)

Boil 2 cups of the sparkling tea in a small saucepan over high heat.

Meanwhile, in a large mixing bowl, combine the remaining 2 cups tea with the gelatin. Let it stand for 2 minutes. Stir the mixture, then add the boiling tea. Using a whisk, continue mixing until the gelatin is completely dissolved. Pour the mixture into an 8" x 8" glass baking dish. Let stand to cool for 15 minutes. Cover the dish with plastic wrap. Refrigerate for 5 hours, or until firm.

Cut the gelatin into 1" cubes (see note below). Arrange the cubes in each of 4 martini or wine glasses. Top each with a cherry, if desired. Serve immediately or cover with plastic wrap and refrigerate for up to 3 days.

Note: Alternatively, you and your kids can make fun shapes by using a cookie cutter to cut the gelatin.

Makes 4 servings

Per serving: 25 calories, 6 g protein, 0 g carbohydrates (0 g sugar), trace fat, 0 g saturated fat, 0 mg cholesterol, 0 g fiber, 14 mg sodium

CHOCOLATE RASPBERRY DESSERT PIZZA

I often host parties to watch my favorite TV shows—friends love it when I invite them over on The Biggest Loser *night and make* Biggest Loser *fare. This pizza is a popular ending to the evening. I prepare them as the weigh-ins take place, and they usually vanish before the eliminated contestant is even announced!*

1 reduced-fat whole wheat flour tortilla (7" diameter) (see note)

1 tablespoon + 1 teaspoon Chocolate "Fudge" Sauce (page 215)

1 cup fresh raspberries

Preheat the oven to 400°F.

Place the tortilla on a small, nonstick baking sheet. Bake for 3 to 4 minutes per side, watching carefully, or until completely crisp through. If air bubbles form during baking, open the oven, poke the bubble with a fork, then use a spatula or oven mitt to press the air out. Transfer the tortilla to a serving plate. Spread 1 tablespoon of fudge sauce evenly over the tortilla, leaving about a ½" border, as you would if you were putting pizza sauce on a traditional pizza.

Arrange the raspberries evenly over the chocolate. Warm the remaining 1 teaspoon of chocolate sauce in the microwave for 5 seconds. Drizzle it over the raspberries. Carefully slice the pizza into four wedges and serve immediately.

Note: I don't recommend using a low-carb tortilla in this recipe. Look for a whole grain or whole wheat option that is low in fat and about 110 calories. The low-carb ones won't crisp properly in the oven and won't taste right either.

Makes 1 serving

Per serving: 220 calories, 5 g protein, 56 g carbohydrates (14 g sugar), 2 g fat, trace saturated fat, 0 mg cholesterol, 11 g fiber, 136 mg sodium

WARM STRING CHEESE ROLLS WITH APRICOT SAUCE

One of the things I most love about this dessert is that there are 8 grams of protein to only 20 grams of carbohydrates. So not only is it delicious, but it's also really satisfying, and you'll feel full after eating a serving.

When you're assembling these rolls, it's really important to make sure there are no holes in your dough rectangles, as you don't want the cheese to ooze out too early in the baking process and burn. That said, even if you do manage to create the "perfect" rectangles, some cheese may bubble out toward the end of the baking. That's okay. The whole point is to create an ooey-gooey delicious treat!

Butter-flavored cooking spray

4 ounces whole wheat pizza dough (no more than 3 grams of fat per 2-ounce serving)

4 sticks (0.75 ounce each) light string cheese

½ teaspoon coconut sugar

2 tablespoons + 2 teaspoons 100% fruit apricot spread

Preheat the oven to 450°F. Line a small baking sheet with parchment paper. Lightly mist the parchment paper with cooking spray. Half-fill a small bowl with cold water and set it aside.

Cut the dough into 4 equal portions (1 ounce each). Place one portion of the dough on a cutting board or clean, flat work surface. Using your fingers, push the dough into a rectangle that is 4½" long and 3" wide (the rectangle should be positioned so that the longer side lays horizontally). Place the string cheese at the edge of the rectangle closest to you. Tightly roll the string cheese in the dough, then dip your fingertips in the bowl of water and dab them on the dough to seal the sides and edges (it should be tightly sealed). With your fingers flat on top of the roll, gently roll the wrapped string cheese back and forth on the cutting board to tightly seal the seams.

Sprinkle ⅛ teaspoon sugar across about 4" of the cutting board. Roll the wrapped string cheese evenly in the sugar. Place it on the prepared baking sheet. Repeat with the remaining dough, string cheese, and sugar, placing them on the baking sheet a couple of inches apart.

Bake for 7 to 9 minutes, or until the dough is golden brown on the outside and cooked inside (the cheese should be melted on the inside by that point).

Add the fruit spread to a microwaveable bowl and microwave on medium power for 10 to 20 seconds until warmed and melted slightly.

Place each roll on a small serving plate and drizzle each with one-quarter of the apricot spread (about 2 teaspoons on each). Serve immediately.

Makes 4 servings

Per serving: 144 calories, 8 g protein, 20 g carbohydrates (6 g sugar), 3 g fat, 2 g saturated fat, 10 mg cholesterol, 1 g fiber, 280 mg sodium

Ada Wong, Season 10

To keep myself going, I visualize what my life will be like after I reach my goal weight. And during tough workouts, I focus on an object in front of me. It helps to clear my mind and get me through the workout.

RED, WHITE, AND BLUE PARFAIT

This parfait is perfect in the summer when berries are at their peak of freshness. They can be packed in resealable containers for picnics and barbecues or stored as individual servings in a single layer in a big bucket or tub of ice for your guests to pick up as they please. At home, keep them in your refrigerator so the kids can grab a nutritious snack on the way to soccer practice or dance class.

⅓ cup fat-free, fruit juice–sweetened strawberry yogurt (I used Cascade Fresh)

2 tablespoons whole grain, crunchy, high-fiber, low-sugar cereal (I used Kashi 7 Whole Grain Nuggets)

⅓ cup blueberries

⅓ cup fat-free, fruit juice–sweetened vanilla yogurt (I used Cascade Fresh)

⅓ cup sliced strawberries

Spoon the strawberry yogurt into a 12-ounce plastic to-go cup with a lid or a medium resealable plastic container. Top it evenly with 1 tablespoon of the cereal, followed by the blueberries. Repeat with the vanilla yogurt, the remaining 1 tablespoon cereal, and the strawberries. Serve immediately, or cover and store in the refrigerator for up to 1 day.

Makes 1 serving

Per serving: **205 calories, 11 g protein, 41 g carbohydrates (23 g sugar), < 1 g fat, trace saturated fat, 0 mg cholesterol, 4 g fiber, 146 mg sodium**

Sophia Franklin, Season 10

I make a sweet-and-savory snack by mixing about ¼ cup of unsalted raw pecans with a little cinnamon, nutmeg, Truvia, and cayenne pepper. Then I put the nuts on a small baking sheet and pop them in the toaster oven at 450°F for about 3 to 5 minutes.

5

Easy Treats

Originally, we were going to call this chapter "No-Bake Treats," but Chef Devin Alexander crafted some deceptively simple treats that require a little oven time, such as the Ooey Gooey Berry Bakes (page 110), so you may have to turn on your oven for a few minutes to create a few of these delicious recipes. But the treats that come out of the oven are well worth the wait.

Many of these simple sweets also incorporate a healthy serving of fruit—such as the Bearymelon "Cookies" (page 102) and the Hot-to-Trot Honey Lime Melon Bowl (page 105). The Cherry-Vanilla Almond Parfait (page 109) not only packs a fruit punch, but it also contains a whopping 12 grams of protein, making it a satisfying snack before or after the gym.

Season 10 at-home contestant Shanna Masten says she likes to satisfy her sweet tooth with a boost of protein in the form of a frosty shake. She blends together one scoop of *Biggest Loser* protein powder, 1 cup of almond milk, 1 frozen banana, and a packet of stevia. For a little something special, she adds 1 teaspoon of cocoa powder. "Treats like this save me from indulging in something bad," says Shanna.

Jen Eisenbarth of Season 3 says she has a favorite easy no-bake treat that her kids love, too. "To make my absolute favorite go-to sweet, I simply mix together 1 can of pure pumpkin (not pumpkin pie filling) with a 24-ounce container of vanilla fat-free yogurt. I just gently fold the yogurt into the pumpkin and then sprinkle on some cinnamon and nutmeg. Then I chill the whole thing in the freezer for a few hours. You can add crumbled graham crackers or crushed raw pecans on top if you want. I haven't met a kid who doesn't like it. It tastes like pumpkin pie without all the guilt!"

TEAM ORANGE PANNA COTTA

I find this panna cotta particularly filling and satisfying given that it has just over 100 calories and is virtually fat free. If you're a big fan of orange-flavored dessert, it's a must-try treat. Try making it in a heart-, star-, or square-shaped ramekin for a really fun, impressive presentation.

Butter-flavored cooking spray

4 tablespoons orange juice concentrate, defrosted

2 tablespoons fat-free evaporated milk

1 packet (0.25 ounce) unflavored gelatin

1½ cups fat-free, fruit juice–sweetened orange or orange cream yogurt

¼ teaspoon orange extract

Lightly mist four 3½"-diameter (½-cup capacity) ramekins or ½ cup custard dishes with cooking spray.

Combine 2 tablespoons of the juice concentrate and the milk in a very small saucepan. Sprinkle the gelatin over top. Set it aside.

In a medium mixing bowl, mix the yogurt, extract, and the remaining 2 tablespoons of juice concentrate. Set it aside.

Place the gelatin mixture over low heat and stir it constantly with a wooden spoon, breaking apart any chunks of gelatin as you do, until the gelatin is completely dissolved. Pour the mixture into the yogurt mixture and stir until well combined. Divide it evenly among the prepared ramekins and let them stand for 5 minutes. Cover each with plastic wrap and refrigerate them for at least 4 hours until set and chilled. Using a butter knife, carefully scrape around the edges of the ramekins. Turn each panna cotta onto a dessert plate.

Makes 4 servings

Per serving: 104 calories, 6 g protein, 19 g carbohydrates (17 g sugar), trace fat, trace saturated fat, 0 mg cholesterol, trace fiber, 65 mg sodium

Biggest Loser Trainer Tip: Jillian Michaels

Interval training is a vital part of a well-rounded fitness plan. If you don't have access to a treadmill, walk-back sprinting is a great form of interval training you can do outside. All you have to do is sprint for a short distance of 50 yards, then walk back to where you started and repeat.

PEANUT BUTTER CUP PINWHEELS

Every time I go to The Biggest Loser *Ranch, I'm stopped by contestants who want to know how they can satisfy their cravings for chocolate and peanut butter without breaking their calorie budgets. I can certainly relate! How can anyone expect anyone to give up this classic combo forever? Now you don't have to.*

Be sure to use either peanut butter that you or someone at your local natural food store ground from fresh peanuts or a jarred brand that contains only peanuts.

---

1 reduced-fat low-carb whole wheat flour tortilla (7½" diameter)

½ tablespoon 100% peanut butter

1 tablespoon Chocolate "Fudge" Sauce (page 215)

Warm a tortilla by placing it in a preheated medium nonstick skillet large enough for the tortilla to lay flat, for about 20 to 30 seconds (no need to add any fat to the skillet). Transfer the tortilla to a cutting board. Spread the peanut butter in a 3"-wide strip, horizontally, across the center of the tortilla. Then spread the fudge sauce evenly over the whole tortilla (not just over the 3" strip).

Roll the tortilla tightly into a tube, beginning at the point closest to you and rolling away from you (the strip of peanut butter should run the length of the tube). Slice the tube into 8 equal pieces. Arrange the pieces on a serving plate, spiral sides up. Serve immediately.

Makes 1 serving

Per serving: 205 calories, 5 g protein, 37 g carbohydrates (11 g sugar), 6 g fat, < 1 g saturated fat, 0 mg cholesterol, 3 g fiber, 135 mg sodium

Abby Rike, Season 8

It's never too late to make a change for the better in your life, no matter where you are or where you are coming from. You choose how you respond to what life sends you. And there is always hope.

FROZEN S'MORES

It seems impossible that s'mores could ever be made with all-natural ingredients. After all, most marsh-mallows at the supermarket contain little more than corn syrup. But we found a way! It's helpful to freeze the whipped topping before you spread it on the graham crackers (don't worry, it doesn't get hard, even directly from your freezer). This classic treat is sure to be as big a hit with your little "campers" as they are with the Biggest Loser *"ranchers."*

4 whole wheat organic honey graham cracker sheets (I used New Morning Organic Honey Grahams)

½ cup "Cut the Crap" Whipped Topping (page 217), preferably frozen

2 tablespoons Chocolate "Fudge" Sauce (page 215)

Break each graham cracker in half (so each half is a square). Spread 2 tablespoons whipped topping evenly over the inside of each of 4 halves. Spread ½ tablespoon fudge sauce evenly among the insides of the 4 remaining halves. Very gently, sandwich the crackers together to form 4 sandwiches, each with a layer of whipped topping and a layer of fudge sauce. Transfer the sandwiches to an airtight plastic container and store them in the freezer. Freeze for about 2 hours or up to 1 month. Serve frozen.

Makes 4 servings

Per serving: **155 calories, 2 g protein, 30 g carbohydrates (14 g sugar), 3 g fat, trace saturated fat, 0 mg cholesterol, trace fiber, 163 mg sodium**

Sam Poueu, Season 9

Everything you're doing is for you and the betterment of you. YOU are what this journey is all about. When I first came to the Ranch, my mission was to defeat my mental barriers. There's no better feeling than accomplishing what you set out to do each day. The self-confidence you will feel as a result is amazing.

KICK BUTT TROPICAL KEBABS

It's amazing how much the flavor of fruit changes when you grill it. A skewer of peaches and pineapples doesn't exactly feel like dessert to me, but the heat from the grill brings out its natural sweetness and makes it drippy and juicy (a true sign of decadence, if you ask me). The addition of the coconut takes it a step further to create this clean, satisfying everyday dessert.

2   firm medium peaches

16   1½"-cubes fresh pineapple

2   teaspoons finely shredded reduced-fat unsweetened coconut (I used Let's Do . . . Organic 40% less fat coconut)

You'll need 8 skewers, metal or wooden, at least 8" long. If using wooden, soak them in water for at least 30 minutes.

Preheat a grill to high.

Halve the peaches and remove the pits (see note below). Using a vegetable peeler, peel the skin from each half, then cut each half into quarters, creating 16 cube-like pieces (not slices). Onto each skewer, thread one peach cube then one pineapple cube followed by a second peach cube and a second pineapple cube.

Turn the grill down to medium and place the skewers on the grill (if using a charcoal grill, place the skewers away from the direct flame). Grill the skewers, gently rotating them every 2 minutes, for 6 to 8 minutes, or until the fruit is tender and has grill marks. Carefully transfer the kebabs to a serving platter and sprinkle them evenly with the coconut (about ¼ teaspoon per kebab). Serve immediately.

Note: When cutting a peach in half, cut 90 degrees from the "seam" that runs down the peach, making sure your knife reaches all the way to the pit. Then gently twist the halves in opposite directions. They should come apart easily.

Makes 4 servings

Per serving (2 skewers): 65 calories, 1 g protein, 15 g carbohydrates (8 g sugar), <1 g fat, <1 g saturated fat, 0 mg cholesterol, 2 g fiber, <1 mg sodium

BEARYMELON "COOKIES"

Let's face it, kids (big and small) love cookies. By calling these adorable slices of watermelon "cookies" and decorating them a bit, your kids and their friends are a lot more likely to accept them as an after-school snack. Heck, it's possible word will even get out that you're the cool mom, dad, aunt or uncle on the block, and you'll have kids flocking to your house for these cookies, especially in the summer.

---

6 small or 3 large ½"-thick slices seedless watermelon

6 teaspoons frozen "Cut the Crap" Whipped Topping (page 217) (see note)

Press a 4" × 3" bear-shaped cookie cutter** into the watermelon. If your cookie cutter isn't thick enough, simply press the cookie cutter into the watermelon as far as it will go. Then, using a paring knife, carefully cut around the bear, if it's not completely "free."

Place a very small, round pastry tip in a pastry bag or plastic sandwich bag with a small triangle cut out of one of the bottom corners (if using a plastic bag, be sure that the pastry tip fits very tightly in the hole). Then decorate the "cookie" with the whipped topping by adding ears, a face, a bow tie, hands, and feet, as shown in the photo, or as desired. Repeat with the remaining watermelon and whipped topping. Serve immediately.

Note: Each bear only requires about 1 teaspoon of whipped topping to decorate it as pictured. You might want to have more on hand to make it easy to pipe from your pastry bag.

***You can use any size or shape of cookie cutter. Just note that the nutritional information below is based on a 2½-ounce piece of watermelon.*

Makes 6 cookies

Per cookie: 22 calories, trace protein, 6 g carbohydrates (6 g sugar), 0 g fat, 0 g saturated fat, 0 mg cholesterol, trace fiber, trace sodium

CHOCOLATE PEANUT BUTTER BALLS

It's no secret that I was a yo-yo dieter for years before I became a "weight-loss success story." I always joked that I was so creative with food that I could turn anything "good" into something "bad." When I first started making these chocolate peanut butter balls using a slightly different recipe, I got hooked and couldn't stop eating them. So I've tweaked these slightly, swapping cocoa powder for carob powder because I like the chocolatey taste even better. I still absolutely love these, but I'm careful not to overdo it; I suggest you do the same.

½ cup + 2 tablespoons old-fashioned oats

2 tablespoons honey

2 tablespoons unsweetened cocoa powder

1 tablespoon unsweetened all-natural creamy peanut butter

Add the oats, honey, cocoa powder, and peanut butter to a medium mixing bowl. Using an electric mixer fitted with beaters, mix until well combined. Lay a large square of waxed paper on a cutting board or flat work surface. Using your hands, divide the mixture into 8 equal portions (the mixture will be sticky), and place on the paper. Roll each portion into a ball. Serve immediately or store on the countertop in a resealable plastic container for up to 3 days.

Makes 8 balls

Per ball: 56 calories, 2 g protein, 10 g carbohydrates (4 g sugar), 2 g fat, trace saturated fat, 0 mg cholesterol, 1 g fiber, trace sodium

Bette-Sue Burklund, Season 5

Everybody's journey is different. Just be committed to your goal, track your calories, and be more active today than you were yesterday.

HOT-TO-TROT HONEY LIME MELON BOWL

In some parts of Los Angeles, it's easy to find fruit carts where the freshest fruit in season is sold. The cart owners often sprinkle lime juice and cayenne pepper over pineapple, honeydew, or cantaloupe. This slightly sweeter version of honeydew is surprisingly refreshing. If you like a little heat, feel free to sprinkle it with some cayenne pepper before serving.

---

2   **teaspoons freshly squeezed lime juice**

¼   **teaspoon fresh lime zest**

1   **teaspoon honey**

1½   **cups cubed honeydew**

In a small bowl, whisk together the lime juice, lime zest, and honey until well combined.

Add the melon to a resealable plastic container. Drizzle the dressing evenly over top and toss well to coat. Cover and refrigerate for 1 hour. Serve immediately.

Makes 1 serving

Per serving: 116 calories, 1 g protein, 30 g carbohydrates (26 g sugar), trace fat, trace saturated fat, 0 mg cholesterol, 2 g fiber, 46 mg sodium

Ashley Johnston, Season 9 Finalist

My nutrition habits have definitely changed. I used to eat out a lot—fried foods, alcohol, lots of high-calorie stuff. Now I cook every single meal. I make healthy substitutes like Truvia in place of sugar, salt-free seasonings in place of sodium, wheat pasta instead of white pasta. I've learned to live healthier, and I love it!

OOEY GOOEY BERRY BAKES

Before starting these bakes, be sure that your berries are completely defrosted and that you do not discard any juice that's released in the defrosting process. The goal is to use that juice as part of the "filling."

---

1 cup frozen mixed berries, defrosted

1 tablespoon honey

¼ cup whole grain, crunchy, high-fiber, low-sugar cereal (I used Kashi 7 Whole Grain Nuggets)

1 tablespoon raspberry, blackberry, or mixed berry 100% fruit spread

2 tablespoons "Cut the Crap" Whipped Topping (page 217), optional

Preheat the oven to 350°F.

In a small mixing bowl, stir together the berries and honey until well combined.

Add the cereal to a resealable plastic bag. Lay the bag on a cutting board or flat work surface. Using the flat end of a meat mallet, pound the cereal to crush it into fine crumbs. Add the crumbs and fruit spread to a small bowl and stir until well combined.

Divide the cereal mixture evenly among two 3½" (½-cup capacity) ramekins. Using the back of a spoon, press the crumbs evenly into the bottoms. Spoon the mixed berries evenly among the ramekins.

Bake for 15 minutes, or until the berries are hot throughout. Allow to cool for 2 minutes. Top each with 1 tablespoon whipped topping, if desired. Serve immediately.

Makes 2 servings

Per serving: 139 calories, 2 g protein, 33 g carbohydrates (18 g sugar), trace fat, 0 g saturated fat, 0 mg cholesterol, 4 g fiber, 65 mg sodium

Biggest Loser Trainer Tip: Bob Harper

If you've had a bad day, week, or weekend, just get back on the wagon. You can always start over today, whatever day today is. Don't stress about what happened in the past; live in the here and now.

OPEN-FACED BANANA ALMOND WAFFLE

I tested this recipe using two different varieties of almond butter. One is a popular brand (Blue Diamond), and the other came from pure almonds that I ground fresh at a natural food store. In the end, everyone in my test kitchen agreed that the Blue Diamond almond butter had a richer, more decadent flavor. Plus, it seemed creamier and easier to spread on the waffle, while the freshly ground butter was a little stiff and difficult to spread. You can use jarred or fresh ground—just be sure that whichever you use is 100 percent almonds with no added sugar or oil.

1 **light whole grain naturally sweetened frozen waffle (no more than 70 calories per waffle; I used Van's Lite 97% Fat-Free Waffles)**

½ **tablespoon almond butter (I used Blue Diamond Homestyle Creamy Almond Butter)**

½ **small banana (about 6"), sliced into ¼"-thick rounds**

Pinch ground cinnamon

Toast the waffle according to package directions. Place the toasted waffle on a small serving plate and spread the almond butter evenly over top. Arrange the banana slices evenly over the waffle. Sprinkle with cinnamon. Serve immediately.

Makes 1 serving

Per serving: 166 calories, 3 g protein, 30 g carbohydrates (8 g sugar), 6 g fat, <1 g saturated fat, 0 mg cholesterol, 5 g fiber, 171 mg sodium

Michael Ventrella, Season 9 winner

When I want to go out for a high-calorie dinner, I compensate ahead of time by working out extra hard. Then I eat an appropriate portion size of the food I want. That's my trick— I'm earning the foods that I want.

CHERRY-VANILLA ALMOND PARFAIT

This parfait looks beautiful and impressive in a parfait glass, but it's also a great on-the-go snack if you construct it in a resealable plastic container. I particularly love it in summer months when cherries are at their peak. In the winter, you can always use frozen cherries—just make sure to find a brand with no added sugar.

⅔ cup fat-free, fruit juice–sweetened, cherry vanilla or vanilla yogurt (I used Cascade Fresh)

1 tablespoon whole grain, crunchy, high-fiber, low-sugar cereal (I used Kashi 7 Whole Grain Nuggets)

½ cup stemmed, pitted, and quartered fresh cherries

1 tablespoon finely chopped lightly salted dry-roasted almonds

Spoon ⅓ cup of the yogurt into the bottom of a parfait or wine glass. Top the yogurt evenly with the cereal, followed by ¼ cup of the cherries. Repeat with the remaining yogurt and cherries. Top with the almonds. Serve immediately or cover with plastic wrap and refrigerate for up to 1 day.

Makes 1 serving

Per serving: 224 calories, 11 g protein, 37 g carbohydrates (25 g sugar), 4 g fat, trace saturated fat, 0 mg cholesterol, 3 g fiber, 128 mg sodium

Jesse Atkins, Season 10

I like making smoothies as a sweet treat. A cup of frozen strawberries, a half cup of frozen raspberries, a cup of milk (I use light vanilla soy milk), a cup of water, and a cup of spinach blended makes a great smoothie. (The spinach doesn't change the taste at all. It's just a great way to get an extra serving of veggies in there.) If you need it to be sweeter, add a packet of Truvia.

6

Frozen Favorites

The great thing about frozen treats is that they're so simple to make, and they take longer to eat since they're cold, so you're less likely to eat them quickly and overindulge. Frozen fruit, icy smoothies, sugar-free ice pops, and frozen yogurt are all cool treats enjoyed by the contestants at the Ranch and at home.

Season 8 winner Danny Cahill says that when he was at the Ranch and got a craving for his favorite dessert—strawberry ice cream—he would whip up a batch of frozen strawberries with almond milk in a blender for a healthy strawberry milkshake. "I often included a scoop of vanilla whey protein mix, too," he says.

Coleen Skeabeck of Season 6 says she has a sweet tooth that just won't quit. Her strategy is to satisfy most of her sweet cravings with healthy alternatives, though sometimes she lets herself indulge in a full-calorie treat. "If I'm having a hard-core craving," she says, "I ask myself: Do I *need* it or *want* it? And if I do choose to eat it, I think about what I'll need to do extra to burn off all of those extra calories." After she indulges in a high-calorie treat, though, she often finds it wasn't even worth all the buildup.

So she's come up with a couple of "faux frozen treats" that satisfy her cravings. For instance, she creates a low-cal frozen "peanut butter cup" by coating a sugar-free Fudgsicle with 1 tablespoon of unsweetened peanut butter. "It's so unbelievably delish," she says.

Chef Devin Alexander suggests that if you really love ice cream and sorbet, it's a good idea to invest in a decent ice cream maker (you can find them these days for about $50). As she points out, when you make it yourself, you have total control over what you're eating—no added sugars can sneak in!

BANANA "ICE CREAM"

When you serve this "ice cream" to your friends and family, they won't believe it only contains one ingredient. It's insane how creamy frozen bananas become when you mix them just enough in your food processor! Just be sure your bananas aren't overripe or underripe. While overripe bananas are great for baked goods like banana bread, they're actually not ideal for ice cream and smoothies. Underripe bananas will taste a bit sour. You want to peel and freeze bananas for this ice cream when they're ripe (yellow with some brown spots) but not overly brown or with any green.

---

2 medium ripe bananas, peeled, frozen (about 7")

Remove the bananas from the freezer and cut them into 1" pieces. (If you don't have frozen bananas, cut fresh, ripe bananas into 1" pieces and place them in an airtight container. Freeze them for at least 1 to 2 hours.)

Add the frozen banana pieces to the bowl of a food processor fitted with a chopping blade. Process until completely smooth, pausing if necessary to scrape down the sides of the bowl. Continue processing the banana until it is slightly aerated and fluffy, about 1 more minute (be careful not to overprocess or the banana mixture will begin to melt and liquefy). Divide the "ice cream" evenly among 2 small dessert bowls. Serve immediately.

Makes 2 servings

Per serving: 110 calories, 1 g protein, 29 g carbohydrates (21 g sugar), 0 g fat, 0 g saturated fat, 0 mg cholesterol, 4 g fiber, 0 mg sodium

Biggest Loser Trainer Tip: Bob Harper

When you're having a bad day and you reach out for something unhealthy to eat, that's when you have to start making changes. If something triggers an unpleasant emotion for you, look for another outlet. You've got to change the reflex of reaching for food.

SUPER SIMPLE CHOCOLATE ICE CREAM

One of the perks of being a chef is that people often send me cool cooking gadgets. Over the past 15 years, I've probably been sent at least 10 ice cream makers, and they've all either collected dust or were donated. I never understood why anyone would spend so much time making something that wasn't much different than the stuff you can get at the store.

But now that I'm committed to creating decadent desserts using only the most natural sweeteners, I've fallen in love with my ice cream maker! It allows me to create ice cream like this one, which is not only three-ingredient-simple but also healthier than any I've found on the market to date.

1 can (12 ounces) fat-free evaporated milk

¼ cup unsweetened cocoa powder

3 tablespoons light agave nectar

Pour ¼ cup of the evaporated milk and the cocoa powder into a medium mixing bowl. Using a whisk, mix the ingredients until very well combined and no lumps remain. Slowly whisk in the remaining milk followed by the agave until well combined and smooth.

Transfer the mixture to the bowl of an ice cream maker that holds at least 2 quarts. Prepare the ice cream according to the manufacturer's directions.

Makes 5 (½-cup) servings

Per serving: 100 calories, 6 g protein, 20 g carbohydrates (17 g sugar), < 1 g fat, trace saturated fat, 3 mg cholesterol, 1 g fiber, 79 mg sodium

Jen Eisenbarth, Season 3

I like eating desserts with a long-handled teaspoon. It not only feels more fun and fancy but also is a nice way to enjoy the dessert longer (by taking smaller bites)!

PINA COLADA SORBET

You'll notice I use small amounts of alcohol, coffee powder, and similar ingredients in numerous recipes throughout this book. At first glance, they may seem insignificant, but please know that I take my desserts very seriously. There are no throwaway ingredients unless they are marked "optional." Trust me, the addition of the ½ tablespoon of coconut rum in this recipe truly matters—it quickly transforms this sorbet into something decadent.

2½ cups frozen pineapple chunks

¼ cup + 1 tablespoon light coconut milk

½ tablespoon coconut rum

2 teaspoons light agave nectar

1 mini pineapple, cut in half and scooped out to make 2 "bowls" (optional)

Place the pineapple chunks in the bowl of a food processor fitted with a chopping blade. Process, stopping to intermittently scrape down the sides of the bowl, if necessary, until the pineapple is finely chopped. Add the coconut milk and process until just smooth. Add the rum, then the agave. Continue processing until well combined (be careful not to overprocess).

Divide the sorbet among the pineapple halves, if desired, or among 2 martini glasses or small dessert bowls. Serve immediately.

Makes 2 servings

Per serving: 150 calories, 1 g protein, 32 carbohydrates (24 g sugar), 3 g fat, 2 g saturated fat, 0 mg cholesterol, 3 g fiber, 5 mg sodium

O'Neal Hampton, Season 9

If you fall off your eating plan, don't beat yourself up. Just go right back to eating healthy. Never get into the place where you say, "Well, I had one piece. I might as well have another and another."

TART RASPBERRY SORBET

I've made this sorbet time after time with store-bought frozen raspberries, and I never thought it was too tart. However, I recently made it with fresh raspberries that I'd frozen myself and found that the sorbet definitely needed a little extra sweetness. I've included an optional addition of agave nectar here because whether or not you need it really will depend on the particular batch of berries you use. If you don't have agave, honey is a great option as well. Either sweetener adds about 20 calories per teaspoon.

1¾ cups frozen raspberries

3 tablespoons fat-free, fruit juice–sweetened vanilla yogurt (I used Cascade Fresh)

2 tablespoons frozen 100% apple juice concentrate (defrosted, if necessary, to measure it)

½ tablespoon fresh lime juice

1 to 2 teaspoons agave nectar (optional)

Place the raspberries in the bowl of a food processor fitted with a chopping blade and process until finely chopped. Add the yogurt, juice concentrate, and lime juice. Process until smooth, intermittently stopping to scrape down the sides of the bowl, if necessary. Add the agave, if desired, and process until just combined (be careful not to overprocess or the sorbet will melt).

Divide among 2 martini glasses, wineglasses, or small dessert bowls and serve immediately.

Makes 2 servings

Per serving: 107 calories, 2 g protein, 24 g carbohydrates (17 g sugar), < 1 g fat, 0 g saturated fat, 0 mg cholesterol, 6 g fiber, 15 mg sodium

MANGO-PEACH KEY LIME SORBET POPSICLES

If you can't find key limes (or if they're too expensive), don't worry. These popsicles can be made with juice from any limes—just don't use bottled lime juice! If you use regular limes, be sure to reduce the amount of juice by half as key limes are sweeter.

To make these popsicles even more fun, try using popsicle molds in different shapes. Tovolo (tovolo. com) makes Rocket Pops, Shooting Stars, and Freezer Gems molds, all of which are a huge hit with kids. If you use other molds, please note that the capacity will be different, so the recipe will likely yield more than 6 pops.

---

2   cups frozen mango chunks

2   cups frozen peach slices

1   cup fat-free, fruit juice–sweetened vanilla or peach yogurt (I used Cascade Fresh)

2   teaspoons honey, or to taste

2   tablespoons freshly squeezed key lime juice

6   popsicle molds (approximately ½-cup capacity)

Add the mango and peaches to the bowl of a food processor fitted with a chopping blade and process until finely chopped. Add the yogurt, honey, and lime juice and process until very smooth and well combined (the mixture should resemble a sorbet).

Spoon the sorbet evenly among 6 popsicle molds, being sure each mold is completely filled. If you see air bubbles forming inside the molds, tap on them lightly so the sorbet gets evenly distributed. Freeze for 6 hours or overnight. To serve, remove the popsicles from the freezer and let them stand for 2 minutes. If the molds don't remove easily, run them under warm water, being careful not to allow water to drip into the popsicles. Serve immediately.

Makes 6 servings

Per serving: 96 calories, 3 g protein, 22 g carbohydrates (19 g sugar), trace fat, trace saturated fat, 0 mg cholesterol, 2 g fiber, 20 mg sodium

COFFEE-TOFFEE GRANITA

Make sure you use a bold coffee to yield the best results in this recipe. Brew it very strong (stronger than you would want to drink it), otherwise the granita could end up tasting watery. And be sure to use a metal pan (not a glass one) so it freezes properly. Don't use your nonstick pans—you need to be able to scrape your pan with a metal fork, and you don't want to scratch the coating.

Because this granita has only 1 calorie, it's a true option anytime.

---

2   cups double-strong brewed room-temperature toffee-flavored coffee (I used Don Francisco's Butterscotch Toffee Flavored Coffee)

20 drops English Toffee Liquid Stevia (I used SweetLeaf), or to taste

Using a whisk, mix the coffee and stevia in a medium mixing bowl, until well combined. Pour the mixture into a 9" × 13" metal pan. Place the pan in the freezer, making sure the pan sits level. After 20 minutes, remove the pan from the freezer and scrape ice crystals from the bottom and sides of the pan using a dinner fork. Return the pan to the freezer. Continue the process of scraping the ice crystals every 20 to 30 minutes, returning the pan to the freezer immediately after scraping, for 2 to 3 hours.

When the coffee mixture is completely frozen, scrape the pan one last time, breaking the granita into small, fluffy flakes. Place the pan back in the freezer for 30 minutes to 1 hour, or until the granita flakes are fluffy and dry (no liquid should remain anywhere in the pan). Divide the granita among 4 margarita glasses or small dessert bowls and serve immediately.

Makes 4 (approximately 1-cup) servings

Per serving: 1 calorie, trace protein, 0 g carbohydrates (0 g sugar), trace fat, 0 g saturated fat, 0 mg cholesterol, 0 g fiber, 2 mg sodium

CHOCOLATE PUDDING POPS

This recipe makes four ½-cup popsicles, but if you have fancy popsicle molds that make five, each will simply hold a little less of the mixture. That's okay—you'll have an extra popsicle, and each will contain fewer calories. If you divide the mixture evenly among five molds, each popsicle will have 123 calories and less than 1 gram of fat.

Any time you are heating a mixture that contains milk on the stove top, be sure to stir constantly to prevent burning.

---

2 cups fat-free milk

⅓ cup nonfat dry milk powder

⅓ cup coconut sugar

3 tablespoons unsweetened cocoa powder

1 tablespoon cornstarch

Place a medium nonstick saucepan over medium heat. Add the milk, milk powder, sugar, cocoa, and cornstarch. Cook the mixture, stirring constantly, for 16 to 18 minutes, or until it thickens to the consistency of gravy. Allow the mixture to cool to room temperature.

Spoon the mixture evenly among four ½-cup capacity popsicle molds (five ⅓-cup capacity popsicle molds is another option). Tap them lightly so the mixture evenly distributes in the molds. Freeze them for at least 6 hours or overnight. To serve, remove the popsicle molds from the freezer. Let them stand at room temperature for 2 minutes, then run them under warm water, if necessary (being careful not to let the water drip into the filling), to remove the molds. Serve immediately.

Makes 4 servings

Per serving: **153 calories, 8 g protein, 30 g carbohydrates (20 g sugar), <1 g fat, trace saturated fat, 3 mg cholesterol, <1 g fiber, 140 mg sodium**

MEXICAN "FRIED" ICE CREAM

This treat is a great way to get your kids in the kitchen. The ice cream balls taste best if you eat them very soon after making the ice cream. If the ice cream is not hard enough when it emerges from your ice cream maker, freeze it for about 20 minutes before coating the balls.

Be sure to have all of your ingredients prepped before you start assembling this dessert. The ice cream melts quickly, so you'll want to have everything ready to go!

⅔ cup fruit juice– or molasses-sweetened whole oat or whole grain cinnamon cereal (I used Barbara's Bakery Cinnamon Crunch Shredded Oats Cereal)

1 cup Tart Honey Vanilla Frozen Yogurt (page 128)

1½ teaspoons honey

Ground cinnamon, to taste

Place the cereal in a resealable plastic bag. Place the bag on a cutting board or flat work surface and, using the flat end of a meat mallet, crush the cereal into coarse crumbs. Place the crumbs on a small plate.

Using a 1¼" ice cream scoop, scoop the frozen yogurt into six 1¼" diameter balls. Working quickly, carefully roll the ice cream balls, one at a time, in the cereal until they are coated (you will have some cereal left over). Transfer the coated ice cream balls to a resealable plastic container. Proceed to the next step immediately or freeze for 5 to 15 minutes, or until they harden slightly.

Place 2 ice cream balls in a small serving bowl. Drizzle ½ teaspoon honey over them, then sprinkle them generously with cinnamon (sprinkle some cinnamon around the plate, too, for dipping). Repeat with the remaining balls, honey, and cinnamon. Serve immediately.

Makes 3 servings

Per serving: 115 calories, 7 g protein, 21 g carbohydrates (15 g sugar), trace fat, trace saturated fat, 0 mg cholesterol, trace fiber, 50 mg sodium

HAND-STAND KIWI STRAWBERRY BANANA SPLIT

If you're in a hurry and don't want to get fancy, you can prepare this banana split like any other or even just combine the ingredients in a bowl. But when you serve this "stand up" banana split in a trifle dish, you give it a unique spin that makes it feel more special.

1 firm small banana, peeled and halved lengthwise (about 6")

⅓ cup Tart Honey Vanilla Frozen Yogurt (page 130)

1 tablespoon chopped strawberries

1 tablespoon peeled and chopped kiwi

1 tablespoon Chocolate "Fudge" Sauce (page 215)

1 to 2 tablespoons "Cut the Crap" Whipped Topping (page 217), optional

Cut the banana halves in half crosswise, creating 4 banana pieces. Stand the banana pieces, cut sides facing inward, spacing them evenly around the edges of a miniature trifle dish or small decorative bowl or glass. Scoop the frozen yogurt in the center of the dish (in the middle of the banana slices). Sprinkle the strawberry and kiwi pieces over the yogurt. Drizzle the fudge sauce evenly over top. Top with whipped topping, if desired. Serve immediately.

Makes 1 serving

Per serving: 207 calories, 7 g protein, 47 g carbohydrates (33 g sugar), < 1 g fat, trace saturated fat, 0 mg cholesterol, 3 g fiber, 27 mg sodium

Julie Hadden, Season 4

I was that girl who sat on her couch watching *The Biggest Loser* with a bucket of nachos in front of me. And now that I've lost the weight, I have to be honest—making the right choices every day doesn't stop. This is the rest of your life. You have to make the healthy decisions *most* days. This is a lifestyle change. It's a journey, not a destination.

CHOCOLATE-ALMOND-COCONUT ICE CREAM SUNDAE

When I was a kid, we used to go to Friendly's for a treat after swim meets. During the summer months only, they had a coconut fudge-swirl ice cream that I loved. I've never stopped missing that combo, so I created this sundae that is sure to be loved by others who enjoy the perfect pairing of coconut and chocolate.

½ cup Super Simple Chocolate Ice Cream (page 113)

1 teaspoon finely shredded reduced-fat unsweetened coconut (I used Let's Do . . . Organic 40% less fat coconut)

2 teaspoons Chocolate "Fudge" Sauce (page 215)

1 tablespoon finely chopped lightly salted almonds

1 tablespoon "Cut the Crap" Whipped Topping (page 217)

Spoon the ice cream into a small dessert bowl. Sprinkle the coconut evenly over top. Drizzle the fudge sauce over the coconut, then sprinkle the almonds over top. Top with whipped topping. Serve immediately.

Makes 1 serving

Per serving: 186 calories, 8 g protein, 31 g carbohydrates (26 g sugar), 5 g fat, 1 g saturated fat, 3 mg cholesterol, 3 g fiber, 96 mg sodium

Jerry Skeabeck, Season 6

When I indulge with an ice cream cone, I adjust my calorie intake for the rest of the day or exercise for an extra 20 minutes in the gym. Being in control means acknowledging my occasional desire for sweets and making adjustments to fit them in.

TART HONEY VANILLA FROZEN YOGURT

This all-natural frozen yogurt is a great substitute for store-bought brands, which are often full of sugar. I recommend making a small batch at a time, because the consistency and flavor are best when fresh. Though you can freeze it and eat it later, it becomes harder and thus less creamy.

I love to add a sprinkle of cinnamon to this yogurt when I'm spooning out a serving—it's delicious and makes for a pretty presentation.

2 cups fat-free plain Greek yogurt

3 tablespoons honey

2 tablespoons light agave nectar

2 teaspoons vanilla extract

Add the yogurt, honey, agave, and vanilla to a medium mixing bowl and stir well to combine. Spoon the mixture into the bowl of an ice cream maker that is at least 2 quarts (see note). Make the ice cream according to the manufacturer's directions. Serve immediately or freeze for harder ice cream.

Note: Some ice cream makers require you to freeze the bowl hours prior to making the ice cream. Be sure to plan accordingly.

Makes 5 (½-cup) servings

Per serving: 120 calories, 9 g protein, 21 g carbohydrates (16 g sugar), 0 g fat, 0 g saturated fat, 0 mg cholesterol, 0 g fiber, 38 mg sodium

Biggest Loser Trainer Tip: Jillian Michaels

Instead of eating the same thing day in, day out, try this. Eat strictly according to plan 2 days a week and moderately 3 days a week. Then give yourself a little slack on the weekends. The opportunity to splurge a bit makes it easier for you to stay on a low-calorie intake for longer periods of time.

MANGO SORBET

I love this sorbet. It tastes so indulgent, it's hard to believe the only ingredient is frozen mango. And it's certainly more affordable than going to an ice cream shop!

You can make as much or as little of this sorbet as you like, based on the chart below. The sorbet is best eaten right away. If you try to freeze it, it will harden.

Frozen mango chunks
(see chart below)

Frozen mango chunks	½-cup servings
1⅔ cups	2
3⅓ cups	4
5 cups	6

Add the mango to the bowl of a food processor fitted with a chopping blade. Process until completely smooth, pausing if necessary to scrape down the sides of the bowl. Continue processing the mango (it will clump into a ball, but just continue processing) for 1 minute, or until it is smooth, slightly aerated and fluffy (be careful not to overprocess, or the mango mixture will begin to liquefy).

Spoon ½-cup portions into martini glasses or dessert bowls. Serve immediately.

Makes 2, 4, or 6 (½-cup) servings

Per serving: 100 calories, 1 g protein, 27 g carbohydrates (23 g sugar), 0 g fat, 0 g saturated fat, 0 mg cholesterol, 3 g fiber, 0 mg sodium

Sione Fa, Season 7

I teach my kids that eating healthy gives us fuel and energy. I want them to live a long, active life!

WAFFLE ICE CREAM SANDWICH

I "waffled" as to whether I should call this one serving or two; in the end, I decided to make it one serving because it is definitely best if you make the ice cream fresh, spread it immediately on the waffles, and enjoy the sandwich right away (as opposed to freezing it and cutting it in half). But this will make a pretty large ice cream sandwich, so feel free to cut it in halves or quarters and share if you are craving a smaller, lower-calorie snack. Also note that this sandwich is delicious with the Banana "Ice Cream" (page 116) as well as the other ice creams and sorbets in this book.

2 **light whole grain naturally sweetened frozen waffles (no more than 70 calories per waffle; I used Van's Lite 97% Fat-Free Waffles)**

½ **cup Super Simple Chocolate Ice Cream (page 113)**

Toast the waffles according to package directions. Allow them to cool completely.

Place one waffle on a serving plate and spread the ice cream evenly over it. Top with the remaining waffle. Serve immediately.

Note: If you are cutting the sandwich, it's best to cut the ice cream–topped waffle in half or quarters, as desired, before adding the top, which should also be cut in halves or quarters before topping.

Makes 2 servings

Per serving: 239 calories, 9 g protein, 53 g carbohydrates (21 g sugar), 3 g fat, trace saturated fat, 3 mg cholesterol, 7 g fiber, 419 mg sodium

Aaron Thompkins, Season 10

When I'm craving something sweet, I like to mix together a little bit of almond butter, 100 percent fruit spread, and Greek yogurt. It's awesome!

Bake Sale Staples

It seems like every other day there's an occasion that calls for a little something sweet—a child's birthday party, a colleague's farewell lunch, a PTA meeting, a church bake sale. Sure, it's easy to sign up for "paper plate duty" or to run to the grocery store and pick up a tray of cookies. But all it takes is a little time and effort to make some truly delicious—and healthy—treats for the people we love.

The sweet treats in this chapter are the perfect answer for just these occasions. Many are portable and can be tucked into lunch boxes, divided into pretty portions for bake sales, or packed into tins and resealable containers for hostess gifts or even just healthy car snacks for the road. Whether you're making Expect More Coconut Macaroons (page 140) or Fudge Swirl Peanut Butter Cupcakes (page 161), your friends, family, and guests are sure to appreciate these goodies much more than a bakery box of cookies or a grocery store sheet cake.

Chef Devin Alexander also points out that because these treats were designed to be portable, they're already divided up into individual serving sizes. "You won't be as tempted to keep nibbling or slicing away at something larger when you have the perfect size already portioned for you," she advises.

The recipes that follow are sure to become crowd-pleasers with the kids and grown-ups in your life.

OUTRAGEOUS ORANGE CUPCAKES

I love these cupcakes in part because they're so low in calories. Where else can you find a full-size, moist cupcake with a burst of fresh flavor (orange, in this case) for under 150 calories—including icing?!

Butter-flavored cooking spray

1 cup whole grain oat flour

¾ teaspoon baking soda

¼ teaspoon baking powder

¼ teaspoon salt

3 large egg whites

½ cup fat-free, fruit juice–sweetened vanilla yogurt

¼ cup agave nectar

2 tablespoons orange juice concentrate

2 tablespoons unsalted butter, melted

1 teaspoon vanilla extract

1 teaspoon orange extract

½ tablespoon dried orange peel

2 cups "Cut the Crap" Whipped Topping (page 217)

2 teaspoons freshly grated orange zest

Preheat the oven to 350°F. Line 8 cups of a standard, nonstick muffin tin with foil cupcake liners (see page xiii). Lightly mist them with spray.

Add the flour to the bowl of a food processor or mini-food processor fitted with a chopping blade and process for 2 minutes.

Place a sifter over a small mixing bowl. Add the flour, baking soda, baking powder, and salt and sift them into the bowl.

In a medium mixing bowl, using a sturdy whisk (or a spatula if you don't have one), mix the egg whites, yogurt, agave, juice concentrate, butter, and extracts until well combined. Stir in the flour mixture until just combined. Then stir in the orange peel. Divide the batter among the prepared muffin cups, filling each cup about two-thirds full.

Bake for 19 to 22 minutes, or until a toothpick inserted in the center comes out dry (a few crumbs are okay). Let them cool completely, then top each with about ¼ cup whipped topping, spreading it evenly over the tops. Sprinkle each with about ¼ teaspoon orange zest.

Makes 8 cupcakes

Per cupcake: **144 calories, 4 g protein, 24 g carbohydrates (17 g sugar), 4 g fat, 2 g saturated fat, 8 mg cholesterol, 1 g fiber, 238 mg sodium**

CRISPY PEANUT BUTTER SQUARES

When I started developing recipes for this book, I asked my Facebook friends what "essentials" they wanted to see included. Among the thousands of responses, there were two recurring items: Rice Krispies Treats and Scotcheroos (scrumptious, peanut butter Rice Krispies Treats topped with butterscotch and chocolate chips). So I created this recipe as a more nutrient-rich version of those favorite desserts. Perfect for bake sales and school lunches, these are sure to become favorites in your home.

Butter-flavored cooking spray

3 cups 100% whole grain crispy brown rice cereal (I used Erewhon brand)

¼ cup coconut sugar

¼ cup light agave nectar

¼ cup + 2 tablespoons unsweetened unsalted all-natural creamy peanut butter

Lightly coat an 8" × 8" baking dish with cooking spray. Place the cereal in a large mixing bowl. Set aside.

Place a medium nonstick saucepan over medium heat. Add the sugar and agave and slowly bring the mixture to a boil. Boil for 1 minute. Reduce the heat to low and add the peanut butter. Stir until the peanut butter is melted and the mixture is well combined.

Pour the peanut butter mixture into the bowl with the cereal. Using a rubber spatula, mix until the cereal is well incorporated. Transfer the mixture to the prepared baking dish and, using a piece of parchment or waxed paper, firmly press the cereal into the pan. Allow to cool completely. Cut into 16 squares. Serve immediately or store in an airtight container for up to 4 days.

Makes 16 servings

Per serving: 83 calories, 2 g protein, 13 g carbohydrates (7 g sugar), 3 g fat, trace saturated fat, 0 mg cholesterol, <1 g fiber, 41 mg sodium

Suzy Preston, Season 2

When I make mini-muffins for my boys, I add a little flaxseed and use egg whites instead of the whole egg.

MINI KEY LIME CHEESECAKE PIES

I first created this recipe in a full-size pie plate, but as a "precautionary measure," I switched to individual ramekins because everyone in my kitchen kept going back for "just a bit more." I've found that when dishes are preportioned, it's a lot less likely you'll be tempted to eat more than one serving.

Butter-flavored cooking spray

⅓ cup whole grain, crunchy, high-fiber, low-sugar cereal (I used Kashi 7 Whole Grain Nuggets)

1 tablespoon + ½ cup light agave nectar

1 cup Yogurt Cheese (page 218)

3 large egg whites

⅓ cup freshly squeezed key lime juice, strained

¼ cup fat-free, fruit juice–sweetened vanilla yogurt (I used Cascade Fresh)

1 tablespoon cornstarch

½ teaspoon vanilla extract

⅛ teaspoon salt

1½ teaspoons key lime or lime zest

Preheat the oven to 350°F. Lightly mist six ¾-cup capacity mini pie dishes or ramekins with cooking spray.

Add the cereal to the bowl of a food processor fitted with a chopping blade. Process it for 15 to 20 seconds, or until the cereal is crushed. Mix the cereal and 1 tablespoon of the agave in a small mixing bowl until well combined (the mixture should be slightly sticky). Divide the cereal mixture evenly among the prepared dishes, about 2 teaspoons in each. Using a small piece of parchment paper, lightly press the cereal mixture into an even layer on the bottom of each pie dish to cover the bottoms. Allow the crusts to rest while you prepare the filling (you must let the crusts firm up slightly or small pieces will come apart once the filling is added).

In a medium mixing bowl, using an electric mixer fitted with beaters, beat the yogurt cheese until it is smooth. Add the remaining ½ cup agave and the egg whites and continue beating just until well combined and smooth. Add the lime juice, yogurt, cornstarch, vanilla, and salt. Slowly beat them in until just combined, being very careful not to overmix. Divide the filling evenly among the pie dishes.

Bake for 14 to 16 minutes, or until almost set in the center. Place the pies on a wire rack to cool to room temperature, then refrigerate for at least 5 hours. Just before serving, top each pie with ¼ teaspoon lime zest.

Makes 6 servings

Per serving: 177 calories, 8 g protein, 38 g carbohydrates (30 g sugar), trace fat, trace saturated fat, 0 mg cholesterol, <1 g fiber, 111 mg sodium

EXPECT MORE COCONUT MACAROONS

If you're a fan of coconut, you're bound to love these macaroons. They're a bit less gooey and buttery than the traditional ones, but that's actually a good thing because it allows true coconut lovers to enjoy the coconut. And you'll save more than 70 calories per macaroon over most traditional macaroons!

Butter-flavored cooking spray

2 large egg whites

2 tablespoons coconut sugar

2 tablespoons light agave nectar

⅔ cup finely shredded reduced-fat unsweetened coconut (I used Let's Do . . . Organic 40% less fat coconut)

Preheat oven to 300°F. Line a medium baking sheet with parchment paper and lightly mist it with spray.

Whisk together the egg whites, coconut sugar, and agave until the sugar is completely dissolved. Stir in the coconut until well combined. Spoon the batter in mounds (about 1 level tablespoon per macaroon) onto the prepared pan, so they do not touch, to make 10 macaroons. Bake for 23 to 25 minutes, or until the macaroons are lightly golden brown. Remove the pan to a wire cooling rack and let them cool about 5 minutes. Transfer them to the cooling rack and allow to cool completely. Serve immediately or store them in a resealable plastic container for up to 5 days.

Makes 10 macaroons

Per serving (2 macaroons): 86 calories, 2 g protein, 13 g carbohydrates (10 g sugar), 3 g fat, 3 g saturated fat, 0 mg cholesterol, 1 g fiber, 33 mg sodium

Nicole Michalik, Season 4

When it comes to dessert, you can't go wrong with the kids' menu. If you go and get ice cream, ask for a child-size cone. You'll save at least 100 calories!

BLUEBERRY CREAM CHEESE "STRUDEL"

Most strudels are traditionally made with phyllo dough. Here I've replaced that with whole wheat pizza dough because whole wheat phyllo is difficult to find in grocery stores—and even if you can find it, it requires a significant amount of added butter to taste great.

This recipe calls for sprinkling the sugar-cinnamon mixture underneath the dough. Since the bottom of the dough is the part that will hit your tongue first, you want it to be sweet. Note that because this strudel is made with fresh dough, it tastes best the same day it's made.

2 cups fresh blueberries

1 tablespoon light agave nectar

1 tablespoon cornstarch

1 teaspoon freshly squeezed lemon juice

1 tablespoon coconut sugar

¼ teaspoon ground cinnamon

1 pound whole wheat pizza dough (no more than 3 grams of fat per 2-ounce serving)

1 recipe Vanilla Cream Cheese Dip (page 219)

1 tablespoon egg substitute

Preheat the oven to 400°F. Line a 9" x 13" baking sheet with a piece of parchment paper that fits snugly inside. To keep the parchment paper from sliding, dab the 4 corners of the pan under the parchment paper with a touch of extra cream cheese or peanut butter. Press the parchment paper into the cream cheese or peanut butter.

Place a medium saucepan over medium heat and add the blueberries, agave, cornstarch, and lemon juice. Cook the mixture, stirring frequently with a wooden spoon, until the cornstarch is dissolved, the blueberries release some of their juices, and the mixture thickens (it should resemble blueberry pie filling). Remove the pan from the heat and let the mixture cool while you prepare the crust.

In a small bowl, mix together the sugar and cinnamon until well combined. Sprinkle about half of the sugar mixture lengthwise in a strip down the center one-third of the prepared baking sheet (so it will be on the bottom of the dough in the end).

Stretch the dough into a rectangle as much as possible before placing it in the pan, with the goal of being able to press it to cover the bottom of pan. Then press it into the pan, stretching it all of the way to the edges, creating an even layer.

Spread the cream cheese dip lengthwise in a strip down the center one-third of the dough, leaving about ½" at either end of the dough bare. Top the cream cheese evenly with the blueberry mixture, making

(continued)

sure the berries cover the cream cheese. Fold the bare sides of the dough up over the filling, leaving 2" of the blueberries still exposed in the middle. Pinch the ends slightly so they're sealed, making sure not to push the filling too much toward the center. Brush the crust with the egg substitute and sprinkle the crust and berries with the remaining sugar mixture.

Bake for 23 to 26 minutes, or until the crust is golden brown and the filling is bubbly and hot throughout. Let the strudel cool to room temperature, then slice it into 10 equal slices with a serrated knife. Serve immediately, or refrigerate in an airtight plastic container for up to 1 day.

Makes 10 servings

Per serving: 171 calories, 4 g protein, 30 g carbohydrates (8 g sugar), 4 g fat, 1 g saturated fat, 8 mg cholesterol, 3 g fiber, 253 mg sodium

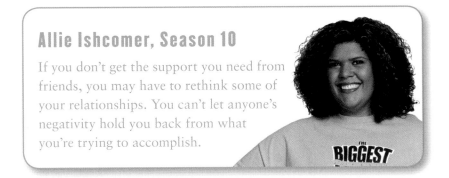

Allie Ishcomer, Season 10

If you don't get the support you need from friends, you may have to rethink some of your relationships. You can't let anyone's negativity hold you back from what you're trying to accomplish.

GO BLUE-BERRY COBBLER MINI LOAVES

These mini loaves make nice gifts and are the perfect sweet taste at breakfast time. If fresh blueberries aren't available, it's fine to use frozen. Just be sure to drain any excess liquid after they've defrosted. All of that purple liquid will change the texture of these otherwise moist and tender loaves.

1 cup old-fashioned oats

¾ cup low-fat buttermilk

Butter-flavored cooking spray

¾ cup + 2 tablespoons whole grain oat flour

1 teaspoon ground cinnamon

1 teaspoon baking powder

¾ teaspoon baking soda

½ teaspoon salt

2 egg whites, lightly beaten

¾ cup + 4 teaspoons coconut sugar

2 tablespoons unsalted butter, softened

¼ cup fat-free, fruit juice–sweetened vanilla yogurt (I used Cascade Fresh)

¾ cup fresh blueberries

In a medium bowl, stir together the oats and buttermilk. Let the mixture stand for 20 to 30 minutes, or until the buttermilk is absorbed.

Preheat the oven to 400°F. Lightly mist 8 individual nonstick loaf pans (3½" × 2½" × 1½") with cooking spray. Set aside.

Add the flour to the bowl of a food processor or mini-food processor fitted with a chopping blade. Process for 2 minutes. Transfer the flour to a sifter. Add the cinnamon, baking powder, baking soda, and salt and sift them into a small mixing bowl.

In a medium mixing bowl, using a sturdy whisk or spatula, mix the egg whites, ¾ cup sugar, the butter, and yogurt until they are well combined and all lumps are removed. Stir in the oat mixture, then the flour mixture until just combined, being careful not to overmix. Fold in the blueberries.

Divide the batter evenly among the prepared pans (about ⅓ cup in each). Sprinkle ½ teaspoon sugar evenly over the top of each loaf. Bake for 13 to 15 minutes, or until a toothpick inserted in the center comes out dry (a few crumbs are okay). Place the loaves on a wire cooling rack to cool for 15 minutes. Then carefully invert the loaves on the cooling rack.

Makes 8 loaves

Per loaf: 202 calories, 5 g protein, 40 g carbohydrates (19 g sugar), 4 g fat, 2 g saturated fat, 9 mg cholesterol, 2 g fiber, 403 mg sodium

CHEAT-NO-MORE APPLE CHEDDAR MUFFINS

I am a true-blue dessert lover. And if it weren't for muffins like these (that I like to consider "breakfast dessert"), I'd be in trouble. These muffins are a bit less sweet than some of the cupcakes in the book, and they're only 150 calories. I like to enjoy them after an egg white omelet or scramble in the morning that's about 150 to 200 calories. That way, I've had a super-filling, extra-satisfying breakfast that's well-balanced for about 350 calories. What better way to start a day?

Butter-flavored cooking spray

1 cup whole grain oat flour

½ cup whole wheat pastry flour

1 teaspoon baking soda

1 teaspoon baking powder

½ teaspoon salt

4 large egg whites

½ cup unsweetened vanilla almond milk

¼ cup 100% apple juice concentrate, defrosted

1 tablespoon + 2 teaspoons canola oil

2 tablespoons fat-free, fruit juice–sweetened vanilla yogurt (I used Cascade Fresh)

½ cup + 1 tablespoon coconut sugar

¾ cup quick oats

¾ cup peeled and minced Granny Smith apple

⅔ cup shredded reduced-fat sharp Cheddar cheese

Preheat the oven to 400°F. Line 12 cups of a standard nonstick muffin tin with foil or silicone cupcake liners (see page xiii). Lightly mist the liners with cooking spray.

Add the flours to the bowl of a food processor fitted with a chopping blade. Process for 2 minutes. Add the flours, baking soda, baking powder, and salt to a sifter and sift them into a medium mixing bowl.

In a large mixing bowl, using a sturdy whisk or spatula, mix together the egg whites, milk, juice concentrate, oil, yogurt, and ½ cup sugar until well combined. Stir in the flour mixture until it is completely incorporated (do not overmix). Stir in the oats, apples, and cheese until just combined.

Divide the batter evenly among the prepared muffin cups (each should be about two-thirds full). Sprinkle the remaining sugar evenly over the muffins (about ¼ teaspoon on each). Bake for 13 to 16 minutes, or until a toothpick inserted in the center comes out dry (a few crumbs are okay). Cool on a wire cooling rack in the pan for 10 minutes. Then remove the muffins onto the rack and allow them to cool. Serve immediately or refrigerate in a resealable plastic container for up to a day.

Makes 12 muffins

Per muffin: 156 calories, 5 g protein 25 g carbohydrates (10 g sugar), 4 g fat, 1 g saturated fat, 4 mg cholesterol, 2 g fiber, 324 mg sodium

Jessica Delfs, Season 10

I walk 6 miles in the morning to burn calories and boost my metabolism for the whole day. It also starts off my day on a peaceful note.

CHOCOLATE HAZELNUT RICOTTA CALZONES

This recipe was inspired by a conversation I had with my physical therapist, Chris, who told me about a more indulgent version of these calzones he'd had in Italy. I saw it as the perfect opportunity to remake it as a protein-rich dessert with significantly fewer calories. These are really best served warm, so if you plan to pack them up and take them on-the-go, be sure to reheat them before serving.

Butter-flavored cooking spray

2 tablespoons + 2 teaspoons Chocolate Sauce (page 214)

1 tablespoon + 1 teaspoon natural dry-roasted hazelnut butter (hazelnuts should be the only ingredient on the label)

½ cup all-natural low-fat ricotta cheese

8 ounces whole wheat pizza dough (no more than 3 grams per 2-ounce serving)

1 tablespoon egg substitute

1 tablespoon + 1 teaspoon agave nectar

Preheat the oven to 450°F. Line a small baking sheet with parchment paper. Lightly mist the parchment paper with cooking spray.

In a small mixing bowl, mix the chocolate sauce and hazelnut butter until well combined. Remove 1 tablespoon plus 1 teaspoon of the mixture to a small bowl and set aside. Add the ricotta to the mixing bowl and stir until well combined.

Place the dough on a cutting board or flat work surface and divide it into 4 equal portions (2 ounces each). Take one portion and press it into a circle that is 6" in diameter. Spoon one-quarter of the ricotta mixture in an even layer over half of the circle, leaving the edges bare. Fold the bare half of the dough over the filled half so the edges connect, then gently pinch the edges together. Carefully transfer the calzone to the prepared baking sheet, reshaping it if necessary.

Repeat the process with the remaining dough and filling, creating 4 calzones, placing them a couple inches apart on the baking sheet. Using a fork, crimp the sealed edges of each calzone, being careful not

(continued)

to poke the tines into the filling. Brush each lightly with the egg substitute. Gently pierce the center of the calzones with a sharp knife. Bake for 9 to 11 minutes, or until the dough is lightly browned and cooked and the filling is hot.

Meanwhile, add the agave to the bowl with the reserved chocolate hazelnut mixture. Stir to combine.

Divide the calzones among 4 dessert plates. Drizzle them evenly with the chocolate hazelnut sauce. Serve immediately.

Makes 4 servings

Per serving: 242 calories, 9 g protein, 40 g carbohydrates (13 g sugar), 6 g fat, 1 g saturated fat, 10 mg cholesterol, 4 g fiber, 318 mg sodium

O'Neal Hampton, Season 9

Don't pick a date to launch your weight-loss plan. Start right now! Don't wait a day or a week or a month. Do it now in some small way. Small steps will lead to big rewards.

DEVIN'S FOOD LAYER CAKE

If you're like me, you're all too familiar with devil's food cake—and for years, so were my hips! I just couldn't resist the rich chocolate flavor. Finally, I adapted it so I could literally have my cake and eat it, too.

Butter-flavored cooking spray

1 cup unsweetened vanilla almond milk

2 tablespoons white vinegar

1¾ cups whole grain oat flour

1½ cups unsweetened cocoa powder

2 teaspoons instant espresso powder

2 teaspoons baking powder

1 teaspoon salt

½ teaspoon baking soda

8 large egg whites

1½ cups agave nectar

½ cup fat-free, fruit juice–sweetened vanilla yogurt (I used Cascade Fresh)

¼ cup canola oil

1 teaspoon vanilla extract

1 recipe "Cut the Crap" Whipped Topping (page 217)

Preheat the oven to 350°F. Lightly coat two 9" round cake pans with spray (just enough for parchment paper to stick), then line the bottom and sides with parchment paper. Lightly mist the parchment paper with spray.

Add the milk and vinegar to a small bowl. Stir them to combine. Set aside.

Place a sifter over a medium mixing bowl. Sift the flour, cocoa powder, espresso powder, baking powder, salt, and baking soda into the bowl. Set aside.

In a large mixing bowl, using a sturdy whisk or spatula, mix together the egg whites, agave, yogurt, oil, vanilla, and the reserved milk mixture until well combined. Mix in the dry ingredients until no lumps remain (do not overmix).

Divide the batter evenly between the prepared pans. Bake them side by side (not one on top of the other) for 30 to 33 minutes, or until a toothpick inserted into the center comes out dry (a few crumbs are okay). Remove the cakes to a cooling rack and let cool for 10 minutes. Gently flip the cakes out of the pans and onto the cooling rack. Let the cakes cool completely.

(continued)

Place one cake, flat side down, on a platter. Spread 1 cup of the whipped topping over the cake. Top it with the second cake, flat side down. Spread the remaining topping evenly over the top and sides of the cake. Slice the cake into 16 equal wedges, cleaning your knife between each slice. Serve immediately or store it in a large resealable cake carrier in the refrigerator for up to 1 day.

Makes 16 servings

Per serving: 232 calories, 6 g protein, 46 g carbohydrates (34 g sugar), 6 g fat, 1 g saturated fat, 0 mg cholesterol, 4 g fiber, 287 mg sodium

Alfredo Dintem, Season 10

You have to eat! You have to get your metabolism started with breakfast and keep it going with lunch, dinner, and snacks. You have to look at your body as a machine. Keep putting fuel into it.

BRING-IT BANANA BUNDTS WITH CHOCOLATE "GANACHE"

These bundts are an adorable addition to any party or bake sale. They're extra moist and will fool anyone into thinking they're eating full-fat cake. For best results, be sure to use very ripe bananas that are soft (but not mushy).

If you love the shape of these adorable cakes as much as I do, I'd suggest investing in silicone mini bundt pans. I've found that it's much easier to remove the cakes intact than any other pans I've used.

Butter-flavored cooking spray

½ cup whole wheat pastry flour

¼ cup + 3 tablespoons whole grain oat flour

½ teaspoon baking soda

½ teaspoon salt

¼ teaspoon baking powder

¾ cup mashed very ripe banana

¼ cup + 2 tablespoons agave nectar

2 tablespoons fat-free, fruit juice–sweetened vanilla yogurt (I used Cascade Fresh)

1 large egg white

2 tablespoons unsalted butter, melted

3 tablespoons + 1 teaspoon Chocolate "Fudge" Sauce (page 215)

Preheat the oven to 350°F. Thoroughly mist 5 cups (each 4" in diameter and 2" tall) of a mini-bundt cake pan(s) with cooking spray.

Add the flours to the bowl of a food processor or mini-food processor fitted with a chopping blade. Process for 2 minutes, then transfer the flours to a sifter. Add the baking soda, salt, and baking powder and sift the dry ingredients together into a small mixing bowl.

Add the banana, agave, yogurt, egg white, and butter to a medium bowl. Using a sturdy whisk or spatula, mix until well combined, being careful not to overmix. Stir in the dry ingredients until no flour is visible and the ingredients are just combined. Divide the batter evenly among the prepared cups, about ⅓ cup in each. Bake for 19 to 22 minutes, or until a toothpick inserted in the center comes out clean (a few crumbs are okay).

Invert the pan(s) onto a cooling rack and gently remove the cakes. Let the cakes cool completely, then top each one evenly with 2 teaspoons of the fudge sauce. Serve immediately, refrigerate up to 1 day, or freeze up to 2 weeks in a resealable plastic container.

Makes 5 servings

Per serving: 250 calories, 4 g protein, 49 g carbohydrates (31 g sugar), 6 g fat, 3 g saturated fat, 12 mg cholesterol, 3 g fiber, 394 mg sodium

STRAWBERRY-FILLED BROWNIE BITES

These brownies freeze well and are great for bake sales and many other occasions. The recipe can easily be doubled.

If your fruit spread seems at all watery, be sure to drain off any excess liquid before using it in this recipe; otherwise, the mini-bites might overflow.

Butter-flavored cooking spray

2 tablespoons whole grain oat flour

2 tablespoons whole wheat pastry flour

½ cup unsweetened cocoa powder

1 teaspoon instant espresso powder

½ teaspoon baking powder

½ teaspoon salt

4 egg whites

1 cup coconut sugar

2 tablespoons unsweetened applesauce

2 tablespoons canola oil

½ teaspoon vanilla extract

½ cup 100% fruit strawberry spread

Preheat the oven to 350°F. Thoroughly mist two 12-cup nonstick mini-muffin tins with cooking spray.

Add the flours to the bowl of a mini-food processor fitted with a chopping blade and process for 2 minutes. Add the flours, cocoa powder, espresso powder, baking powder, and salt to a sifter and sift them into a small mixing bowl.

In a large mixing bowl, using a sturdy whisk or spatula, mix the egg whites, sugar, applesauce, canola oil, and vanilla until well combined. Add the flour mixture and stir until just combined and no lumps remain (be careful not to overmix). Divide the batter among the 24 muffin cups, filling each about two-thirds full (about 1 tablespoon per cup—do not overfill them or the brownies will spill out of the pan). Carefully drop 1 teaspoon of fruit spread directly in the center of each brownie (do not push the fruit spread down into the brownies).

Bake for 10 to 12 minutes, or until a toothpick inserted as close to the center as possible, without touching the fruit spread, comes out dry. Transfer the pan to a cooling rack and allow them to cool for 5 minutes. Using a butter knife, gently lift the brownies from the muffin tins (if they stick, gently run the knife around the edge of each cup). Allow them to cool for another 10 minutes.

Makes 24 brownies

Per brownie: 68 calories, 1 g protein, 13 g carbohydrates (9 g sugar), 1 g fat, trace saturated fat, 0 mg cholesterol, trace fiber, 84 mg sodium

A-LIST APPLE DANISHES

With each new cast of Biggest Loser *contestants, it seems like there's always one person who can't stop obsessing about how much he or she misses apple pie. When asked why, it's always about the filling— they rarely even mention the crust. These Danishes are a great way to satisfy that craving since they are very much about the filling—in fact, a few contestants have reported liking them better than apple pie!*

I love making these Danishes with nice crisp apples like Granny Smith or Golden Delicious.

Butter-flavored cooking spray

1 large tart apple, peeled and cut into ½" cubes (about 2 cups)

3 tablespoons 100% apple juice

1 tablespoon + 1 teaspoon coconut sugar

½ teaspoon freshly squeezed lemon juice

¼ teaspoon + ⅛ teaspoon ground cinnamon

Pinch ground nutmeg

8 ounces whole wheat pizza dough (no more than 3 grams per 2-ounce serving)

¼ cup Vanilla Cream Cheese Dip (page 219)

1 tablespoon egg substitute

Preheat the oven to 400°F. Line a medium baking sheet with parchment paper. Lightly mist the parchment with cooking spray.

Place a medium nonstick skillet over medium-high heat. Add the apples, apple juice, 1 tablespoon sugar, lemon juice, ¼ teaspoon cinnamon, and nutmeg. Cook the mixture, stirring occasionally, until all of the liquid has evaporated and the apples are tender. Remove the pan from the heat.

In a small bowl, stir together the remaining 1 teaspoon sugar and ⅛ teaspoon cinnamon until well combined.

Place the dough on a cutting board or clean, flat work surface and divide it into 4 equal portions (2 ounces each). Take one of the portions and press it into a circle that is 5" in diameter. Sprinkle the dough with ⅛ teaspoon of the sugar cinnamon mixture. Pick up the dough circle and gently flip it onto the prepared baking sheet, so the sugared side is facedown (reshape the circle if necessary).

Spread 1 tablespoon of the cream cheese dip evenly over the circle, leaving ¾" bare around the edges. Spoon one-quarter of the apple mixture (about ⅓ cup) evenly over the cream cheese layer (it will look similar to a mini-deep dish pizza). Then, starting at 12 o'clock, and moving around the circle, fold the bare edges over the filling in

(continued)

45-degree angles (instead of pulling it straight over the filling) in 5 evenly spaced spots, then crease the folds in the dough.

Repeat the process with the remaining dough, sugar mixture (only using ⅛ teaspoon per crust), cream cheese dip, and apple filling, to create 4 Danishes. Place them in a single layer on the baking sheet. Brush the outsides and edges of the crusts lightly with the egg substitute (you will have some left over). Sprinkle the remaining sugar mixture evenly over the crusts and tops of each Danish. Bake for 12 to 15 minutes, or until the crust is cooked and lightly browned and the filling is hot.

Makes 4 servings

Per serving: 230 calories, 5 g protein, 42 g carbohydrates (14 g sugar), 5 g fat, 2 g saturated fat, 10 mg cholesterol, 5 g fiber, 324 mg sodium

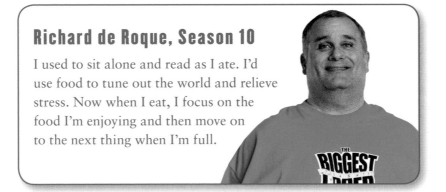

Richard de Roque, Season 10

I used to sit alone and read as I ate. I'd use food to tune out the world and relieve stress. Now when I eat, I focus on the food I'm enjoying and then move on to the next thing when I'm full.

FUDGE SWIRL PEANUT BUTTER CUPCAKES

People always ask me if you can make my cupcake recipes as cakes and my cakes as cupcakes—and the answer is often no. I originally planned this as a cake, but the moistness of the cake coupled with the creaminess of the swirl made the cake rip apart every time I tried to cut it. So I changed the recipe to make these scrumptious, extra-moist cupcakes that you don't have to cut—just bite into!

Butter-flavored cooking spray

⅔ cup whole grain oat flour

½ cup whole wheat pastry flour

1 teaspoon baking soda

1 teaspoon salt

⅓ cup unsweetened all-natural creamy peanut butter

½ cup fat-free, fruit juice–sweetened vanilla yogurt (I used Cascade Fresh)

¾ cup + 2 tablespoons light or blue agave nectar

4 large egg whites

1 teaspoon vanilla extract

¼ cup Chocolate "Fudge" Sauce (page 215)

Preheat the oven to 350°F. Line 12 cups of a standard, nonstick muffin tin with foil or silicone liners (see page xiii). Lightly mist the cups with spray.

Add the flours to the bowl of a food processor or mini-food processor fitted with a chopping blade. Process them for 2 minutes.

Place a sifter over a small mixing bowl. Add the flour mixture, baking soda, and salt and sift them into the bowl.

In a large mixing bowl, using a stand or hand mixer fitted with beaters, cream the peanut butter, yogurt, and agave. Using a heavy whisk or spatula, stir in the egg whites and vanilla. Stir in the flour mixture until well combined. Divide the mixture evenly among the muffin cups (they should each be about two-thirds full). Drizzle 1 teaspoon of the chocolate sauce into the center of each cupcake and, using a toothpick, "swirl" the chocolate into the batter by running the toothpick back and forth through the inside of the cupcake so a swirl pattern is created.

(continued)

Bake for 15 to 18 minutes, or until a toothpick inserted in the center comes out dry (a few crumbs are okay). Cool the cupcakes completely in the pan on a wire rack. Serve or freeze for up to 1 week in an airtight plastic container.

Makes 16 cupcakes

Per cupcake: **181** calories, **5 g** protein, **33 g** carbohydrates (**24 g** sugar), **4 g** fat, **< 1 g** saturated fat, **0 mg** cholesterol, **2 g** fiber, **322 mg** sodium

Stephanie Anderson, Season 9

Watch your alcohol intake! The more you drink, the less inhibited you are around the buffet table. Try alternating an alcoholic drink with a glass of sparkling water or club soda. That will slow down the pace.

8

Healthy Holidays

Ahh, the holidays. When you're losing weight, the prospect of the holidays can conjure up both excitement and dread. After all, what fun is it to go to holiday dinners and parties if you can't indulge with everyone else? And if you do choose to indulge, you know you'll feel guilty the next day and worry that you've undermined all of your hard work.

Well, thanks to Chef Devin Alexander, you can indulge in delicious holiday treats without guilt! Recipes like Pumped-Up Pumpkin Pie Bites (page 172) and Gingerbread Truffles (page 182) are every bit as delicious as the traditional favorites you're used to   and contain just a fraction of the calories.

The Season 9 contestants are facing their first year of holiday temptations, so we caught up with them and asked how they planned to handle the potential temptations. One strategy that many of them said they intended to employ was to bring their own food to gatherings and parties, potluck style.

Cheryl George says she's ultra-careful when she goes to a party and isn't afraid to ask her hostess questions about how the food was prepared. "I'll ask a lot of questions about what went into making the dishes and sample the ones that aren't full of fat, salt, and sugar," she says. Lance Morgan advises, "If you can't bring your own food, and nothing at the party looks very healthy, then it all comes down to portion control. Use a small plate. No seconds. No piling it on the plate."

Koli Palu says he eats before he goes to parties so that he's not famished when gets to the buffet table. "I pick and choose from the lean proteins and the salads. It would be a mistake for me to go there hungry because the temptations to indulge in fat-filled desserts is strong."

Daris George says he navigates tempting situations by trying small portions of several different dishes. It's a way to taste new foods without overdoing it. "It's not required to overindulge," he says. "It's okay to try small amounts of things but you have to make wise choices."

The festive recipes in this chapter offer plenty of options for creating special holiday treats to share with your own guests or to bring to parties. When you make your own treats, you'll always have healthy options to snack on. And once your friends and family members sample them, they'll be glad you did, too!

Thanksgiving: Do You Have to Give Up Pumpkin Pie?

No! says *The Biggest Loser* nutritionist Cheryl Forberg, RD. Modify your favorite recipe with these simple tips.

1. Make pumpkin (or sweet potato) pies with evaporated skimmed milk. It's rich and creamy and contains fewer calories and less fat than regular evaporated milk

2. Try to decrease the amount of sweetener in your favorite recipe by about 25 percent or replace sugar with agave nectar, which is loaded with antioxidants.

3. Increase the amount of spice you add to your pie by just a little. It will enhance the overall flavor and will make the reduced amount of sweetener less noticeable.

4. Substitute most or all of the whole eggs with egg whites.

5. Eat just the filling of the finished pie and skip the high-fat crust. Or, bake the filling in a springform pan without any crust at all!

CARAMEL APPLE BAKE

I used dried apples in this recipe, as they lend a bit more "bite" than fresh apples and create a chewy texture. I wanted this bake to be reminiscent of the flavors of a caramel apple. It's a perfect fall treat, though since the fruit is dried, it can really be made any time of year.

Butter-flavored cooking spray

1 cup whole grain oat flour

½ teaspoon baking powder

¼ teaspoon salt

¾ cup egg substitute

¾ cup coconut sugar

1 teaspoon vanilla extract

¾ pound dried apple rings, cut into small pieces

¼ pound raisins

⅓ cup finely diced walnuts

Preheat the oven to 325°F. Lightly mist an 11" × 7" glass or ceramic baking dish with cooking spray.

In a small mixing bowl, stir together the flour, baking powder, and salt. Set it aside.

In a medium mixing bowl, using a sturdy spatula, mix the egg substitute, sugar, and vanilla. Stir in the flour mixture until well combined, followed by the apples and raisins. Pour the mixture into the prepared baking dish and spread it out evenly. Sprinkle the walnuts evenly over the top.

Bake for 24 to 27 minutes, or until golden brown and a toothpick inserted in the center comes out sticky but not wet. Allow to cool for 5 minutes. Cut into 12 pieces and serve immediately.

Makes 12 servings

Per serving: 210 calories, 4 g protein, 43 g carbohydrates (29 g sugar), 3 g fat, trace saturated fat, trace cholesterol, 4 g fiber, 123 mg sodium

Biggest Loser Trainer Tip: Bob Harper

When it comes to weight loss, loving yourself is key. I have worked with so many people who have been their own worst enemy. It's time to start being your own best friend. When you start putting yourself at the top of your priority list, all your goals will be obtainable.

RAISIN' THE BAR BROWN RICE PUDDING

It's really important that you use short-grain brown rice in this recipe. If you use long-grain, your pudding won't have a nice bite-y texture. Look for frozen brown rice or microwaveable brown rice bowls (see page xx) to make this recipe in a jiffy. Just be sure that the precooked rice you use doesn't contain added ingredients like salt, vegetable broth, or fat.

1½ cups fat-free milk

1 cup fat-free evaporated milk

⅓ cup light agave nectar

2 tablespoons cornstarch

2 large omega-3 eggs, lightly beaten

1 teaspoon vanilla extract

1¼ cups cooked short-grain brown rice

½ cup raisins

Place a medium nonstick saucepan over medium heat. Add the milk, evaporated milk, agave, cornstarch, eggs, vanilla, and rice to the pan. Cook the mixture, stirring constantly, for 5 to 7 minutes, or until it thickens to the consistency of a thick gravy (not quite as thick as a pudding; it will thicken slightly when refrigerated and you don't want it too thick).

Divide the mixture evenly among eight 3½"-diameter (½-cup capacity) ramekins. Divide the raisins evenly among them (about 1 tablespoon on each). Allow them cool to room temperature, then cover and refrigerate the ramekins for 4 hours, or until completely chilled. Just before serving, stir the pudding to distribute the raisins evenly throughout.

Makes 8 servings

Per serving: 179 calories, 6 g protein, 35 g carbohydrates (24 g sugar), 2 g fat, trace saturated fat, 54 mg cholesterol, 1 g fiber, 87 mg sodium

Sherry Johnston, Season 9

There's always lots of finger foods at holiday parties. Most of the time, there will be a vegetable platter, always a smart choice. Just avoid creamy, high-fat dips.

PUMPKIN ICE CREAM

This delicious holiday-inspired ice cream contains just a fraction of the calories and offers a nice dose of protein. When you're cooking the ice cream base on the stove, make sure you scrape down the sides of the pot frequently as you stir. This helps prevent little flecks of the pumpkin mixture from hardening against the side of the pot, leaving you with a smooth, creamy texture.

---

2 tablespoons cornstarch

1 can (12 ounces) fat-free evaporated milk

¼ cup egg substitute

¼ cup 100% maple syrup

3 tablespoons pumpkin puree

¼ teaspoon ground cinnamon

Add the cornstarch to a medium nonstick saucepan. Whisking constantly (using a silicone-coated or plastic whisk, to avoid scratching the pan), add just enough milk to completely dissolve the cornstarch (no lumps should remain). Pour in the remaining milk in a steady stream, as you continue to whisk. Then add the egg substitute, maple syrup, pumpkin, and cinnamon and continue whisking until they are well combined.

Place the pan over medium heat. Cook the mixture, stirring constantly and scraping the edges frequently, for 5 minutes, or until it is smooth and thickens slightly (to the consistency of thick cream). Pour the mixture into a large bowl and allow to cool for 30 to 45 minutes, or until at room temperature.

Spoon the mixture into the bowl of an ice cream maker that is at least 2 quarts. Make the ice cream according to the manufacturer's directions. Serve immediately or freeze for harder ice cream.

Makes 5 (½-cup) servings

Per serving: **121 calories, 6 g protein, 23 g carbohydrates (18 g sugar), trace fat, trace saturated fat, trace cholesterol, trace fiber, 110 mg sodium**

PECAN PRALINE COOKIE THINS

When my Facebook friends learned that I was working on an all-dessert book, I immediately got inundated with requests for re-creating favorite high-cal classics. One of the most popular requests was for pecan pie. These scrumptious cookies, which are ridiculously low in fat and calories compared to pecan pie, are an ode to those requests.

Butter-flavored cooking spray

1 large egg white

2 tablespoons coconut sugar

⅓ cup unsalted dry-toasted chopped pecans (see note)

Preheat the oven to 350°F. Lightly mist 8 cups of a nonstick standard muffin tin with spray.

Whisk together the egg white and sugar until the sugar is completely dissolved. Add the pecans and stir until well combined. Spoon the batter (about a scant 1 tablespoon each) into the prepared muffin tin, making sure to distribute the pecans evenly between each muffin cup.

Bake for 8 to 10 minutes, or until the cookies are lightly crisped around the edges, being careful not to burn them. Cool the tin on a rack for 5 minutes, or until the cookies have cooled slightly. Remove them to a cooling rack and let cool completely. Serve immediately or store in a cookie tin for up to 5 days.

Note: Packages of pecans that say either "dry-toasted" or "dry-roasted" are perfect for this recipe. Just make sure the pecans are not raw—the cookies won't have as much flavor.

Makes 4 servings

Per serving: 95 calories, 2 g protein, 7 g carbohydrates (5 g sugar), 7 g fat, < 1 g saturated fat, 0 mg cholesterol, < 1 g fiber, 27 mg sodium

PUMPED-UP PUMPKIN PIE BITES

These delicious little bites are real crowd-pleasers and are the perfect size for individual servings at a buffet table (instead of asking your guests to cut their own wedge of pie!).

Butter-flavored cooking spray

¾ cup whole grain, crunchy, high-fiber, low-sugar cereal (I used Kashi 7 Whole Grain Nuggets)

2 tablespoons 100% pure maple syrup

¼ teaspoon ground cinnamon

8 large egg whites

1 can (15 ounces) solid pumpkin puree

¾ cup agave nectar

2 tablespoons whole wheat pastry flour

2½ teaspoons vanilla extract

1¼ teaspoons pumpkin pie spice

½ teaspoon baking powder

¼ teaspoon salt

⅔ cup "Cut the Crap" Whipped Topping (page 217), optional

Preheat the oven to 350°F. Lightly mist an 11" × 7" glass or ceramic baking dish with spray.

Add the cereal to the bowl of a food processor fitted with a chopping blade. Process it for 15 to 20 seconds, or until the cereal is crushed. Transfer it to a small mixing bowl and add the maple syrup and cinnamon. Mix them until well combined. Spoon the mixture into the prepared baking dish. Gently press down on the cereal mixture, spreading it evenly across the bottom of the baking dish. Bake for 7 to 9 minutes, or until slightly browned. Set aside.

Meanwhile, add the egg whites to a large mixing bowl. Using a sturdy whisk, lightly beat them until they bubble very slightly. Still using the whisk, stir in the pumpkin, agave, and flour until well combined. Stir in the vanilla, pumpkin pie spice, baking powder, and salt and continue mixing until well combined. Pour the filling over the baked crust. Using a rubber spatula, spread it into an even layer.

Bake for 40 to 45 minutes, or until a toothpick inserted in the center comes out dry (a few crumbs are okay). Transfer the dish to a wire cooking rack, allowing it to cool to room temperature. Carefully cut 32 pumpkin "bites" (3 cuts along the width of the pan, 7 cuts along the length, creating 4 × 8 bites). Just before serving, top each bite with 1 teaspoon whipped topping, if desired. Serve immediately or store in an airtight container in the refrigerator for up to 5 days.

Makes 16 servings (32 bites)

Per serving: 94 calories, 3 g protein, 21 g carbohydrates (15 g sugar), trace fat, trace saturated fat, 0 mg cholesterol, 2 g fiber, 102 mg sodium

Thanksgiving Game Plan

Thanksgiving Day might very well be the ultimate food fest of the year. And while a one-day splurge isn't such a big deal, if you're not careful, it can easily lead to a weekend splurge . . . and eventually, a food free-for-all as all the other fall and winter holidays start to roll around. The BiggestLoserClub.com's Greg Hottinger, RD, and the show's nutritionist, Cheryl Forberg, RD, offer several strategies for enjoying the holidays without veering off course.

Strategy #1: Give Yourself Permission

If the Thanksgiving meal is a special one for you, plan to enjoy it. Make an agreement with yourself that it's okay to have one splurge day. You've worked hard thus far, and enjoying Thanksgiving dinner is not going to ruin all of that work.

Strategy #2: Frame Your Splurge

Limit your indulgences to just the one meal, not the entire weekend. A key to weight-loss success is learning how to keep your exercise program and eating structure healthy the day before and the day after your celebration. This is called "framing" your splurge.

Strategy #3: Have a Plan

To make strategy #2 work, you'll need to plan out the details so that you can stay on track. Can you make sure that you stick to your calorie budget on the Wednesday before Thanksgiving? If you're traveling, can you plan out your exercise for the four-day weekend? Be sure to pack any workout clothing or gear you'll need and be prepared.

Strategy #4: The Splurge

Remember that a holiday meal isn't your last one on planet Earth. How can you maximize your pleasure, fully enjoy the meal, but still feel like you made good decisions? One strategy is to not come into the meal famished. It may be tempting to "starve yourself" before the meal, but that will only set you up for overeating once you sit down to the table. The goal is to have a great time and enjoy your company. Give yourself permission to eat the foods that you love, and savor them.

Strategy #5: Take Pride in Your Recovery

The next day, it's time to get back on track. If you overate, don't beat yourself up about it. If you did well with your choices, then congratulate yourself. Your overall success depends on how quickly you can recover from these special days. If your Thanksgiving normally spills over into Friday and Saturday, can you do it differently this year? It's important to get back on track as quickly as possible and avoid consuming high-calorie leftovers in the coming days.

Overall

Stay hydrated. It's important to drink plenty of water, which transports nutrients and oxygen to your cells and also helps to wash away toxins. Make sure you drink at least eight 8-ounce glasses of water each day. If you drink alcohol at Thanksgiving, increase your water intake to compensate for the dehydrating effects of alcohol. And skip the after-dinner coffee, which can disrupt your sleep cycle, leading to restless nights and decreased energy during the day.

RUN, DON'T WALK, RUM BALLS

These delicious treats contain about half the calories and a tiny fraction of the fat found in traditional rum balls—and as an added bonus, one serving contains 4 grams of fiber!

Make sure you dust the rum balls lightly with cocoa powder. Too much cocoa will impart a bitter taste.

---

1 tablespoon + ¼ cup cocoa powder

1½ cups pitted dates

⅔ cup old-fashioned oats

2 tablespoons dark rum

2 teaspoons vanilla extract

⅛ teaspoon allspice

Add 1 tablespoon of the cocoa to a small bowl and set aside.

Place the dates in the bowl of a food processor fitted with a chopping blade. Process them until they are very finely chopped and stick together. Add the oats, rum, vanilla, allspice, and the remaining ¼ cup cocoa. Continue processing the mixture until the oats are finely chopped and the mixture sticks together (do not overprocess the mixture or it will become extremely sticky and very difficult to work with).

Using a spatula, transfer the mixture to a small mixing bowl or mound it on a cutting board. Divide it into 14 equal amounts (about 1 tablespoon each). Shape each into a ball. Gently roll the balls, one at a time, in the reserved cocoa powder (some excess powder will remain in the bowl). Place them, one at a time, in a fine sieve and gently shake them to remove any excess cocoa powder.

Serve immediately or store them in an airtight plastic container for up to 5 days.

Makes 14 rum balls

Per serving (2 rum balls): 155 calories, 3 g protein, 32 g carbohydrates (7g sugar), <1 g fat, trace saturated fat, 0 mg cholesterol, 4 g fiber, trace sodium

CHOCOLATE ORANGE TRUFFLE RAMEKIN CAKES

These cakes are probably the richest dessert in the book. They're very reminiscent of warm, deep chocolate orange truffles. You would never guess they're low in fat and calories, which is why I love serving these cakes at dinner parties.

Be careful not to let additional extract drip or overflow into these cakes. The ⅛ teaspoon is the perfect amount to flavor them. If you add more, it will overpower the cakes.

Butter-flavored cooking spray

4 large egg whites

⅔ cup light agave nectar

3 tablespoons unsweetened applesauce

½ teaspoon vanilla extract

⅛ teaspoon orange extract

¾ cup unsweetened cocoa powder

½ teaspoon salt

Preheat the oven to 350°F. Mist four 3½"-diameter (approximately ½-cup capacity) ramekins with cooking spray. Place them side by side in an 8" × 8" baking dish and add water to the pan until it reaches halfway up the ramekins.

Add the egg whites, agave, applesauce, vanilla, and orange extract to a medium mixing bowl. Using a sturdy whisk or spatula, mix the ingredients until well combined. Add the cocoa powder and salt and stir until just well combined and no lumps remain, being careful not to overmix.

Divide the batter evenly among the ramekins (each should be about two-thirds full). Bake for 23 to 26 minutes, or until the tops puff slightly and a toothpick inserted in the center comes out just barely wet. Remove the pan from the oven and, using tongs or waterproof oven mitts, carefully transfer the ramekins from the water bath to a cooling rack. Cool for 5 minutes, then serve immediately in the ramekins.

Makes 4 servings

Per cake: 221 calories, 7 g protein, 53 g carbohydrates (44 g sugar), 2 g fat, 1 g saturated fat, 0 mg cholesterol, 5 g fiber, 350 mg sodium

ITTY-BITTY MINTY BROWNIE BITES

The amount of whipped topping yielded from the Fluffy Whipped Topping can vary. It depends on the size of your egg whites and the strength of your electric mixer. You will get at least enough topping to frost each brownie with 1 tablespoon. The nutritional data listed is calculated based on consuming the entire batch of whipped topping among the 24 brownies. Any extra topping can be stored in the freezer for use in another recipe or as a topping to your favorite fruit.

Butter-flavored cooking spray

2 tablespoons whole grain oat flour

2 tablespoons whole wheat pastry flour

½ cup unsweetened cocoa powder

1 teaspoon instant espresso powder

½ teaspoon baking powder

½ teaspoon salt

4 large egg whites

1 cup coconut sugar

2 tablespoons unsweetened applesauce

2 tablespoons canola oil

½ teaspoon vanilla extract

¼ teaspoon peppermint extract

1 recipe Fluffy Whipped Topping (page 182)

Preheat the oven to 350°F. Thoroughly mist two 12-cup nonstick mini-muffin tins with cooking spray.

Add the flours to the bowl of a mini-food processor fitted with a chopping blade and process for 2 minutes. In a small mixing bowl, sift together the flours, cocoa powder, espresso powder, baking powder, and salt.

In a large mixing bowl, using a sturdy whisk or spatula, mix the egg whites, sugar, applesauce, canola oil, and the extracts until well combined. Add the flour mixture and stir until just combined and no lumps remain (be careful not to overmix). Divide the batter among the 24 muffin cups, filling each about two-thirds full.

Bake for 7 to 9 minutes, or until a toothpick inserted in the center comes out dry (a few crumbs are okay). Transfer the pan to a cooling rack and allow them to cool for 5 minutes. Using a butter knife, gently lift the brownies from the muffin tins (if they stick, gently run the knife around the edge of each cup). Allow them to cool completely.

Once they are cool, divide the whipped topping evenly among the brownies (about 1 tablespoon on each), spreading the topping evenly over the top of each. Serve immediately.

Makes 24 brownies

Per brownie: 63 calories, 1 g protein, 13 g carbohydrates (9 g sugar), 1 g fat, trace saturated fat, 0 mg cholesterol, <1 g fiber, 87 mg sodium

1 egg white, at room temperature

¼ cup light agave nectar

⅛ teaspoon cream of tartar

3 to 5 drops green food coloring, as desired

Add water to a medium saucepan until it is about one-quarter full. Bring the water to a boil over high heat.

Off the heat, combine the egg white, agave, cream of tartar, and food coloring in a large metal or heavy-duty glass mixing bowl that will fit onto the top of your saucepan. Using an electric mixer fitted with beaters, beat the mixture on medium to high speed until well blended. Place the bowl over the pot of boiling water. (For safety, be sure to wear an oven mitt while holding the bowl over the heat, as it will get very hot.) Beat for 5 minutes, or until stiff peaks form, occasionally running the beaters around the sides of the bowl to scrape any of the mixture. Remove the bowl from the water and continue beating for 1 minute longer, rotating the bowl and scraping down the sides with the beaters as you do, until the mixture is thick, very fluffy, and has very stiff peaks.

Makes about 1½ cups

Per serving (1 tablespoon): 11 calories, trace protein, 3 g carbohydrates (3 g sugar), 0 g fat, 0 g saturated fat, 0 mg cholesterol, 0 g fiber, 2 mg sodium

Amanda Arlauskas, Season 8

Change your mind-set. If you keep telling yourself you are going to fail, then you *are* going to fail. But if you tell yourself you can do something, then you can. Believing that helped me start running on the treadmill faster than I ever thought I could. Stop the habitual negative thinking.

GINGERBREAD TRUFFLES

This truffle mixture is sticky, so I recommend you remove any rings from your fingers before shaping the truffles. Though the process is messy, the end result is so delicious, you'll quickly agree it's worth it!

1 cup pitted dates

2 tablespoons molasses

¼ teaspoon ground cinnamon

⅛ teaspoon ground ginger

Two pinches ground cloves

Two pinches ground nutmeg

⅔ cup + 2½ tablespoons old-fashioned oats

Place the dates in the bowl of a food processor fitted with a chopping blade. Process them until they are very finely chopped and stick together. Add the molasses, cinnamon, ginger, cloves, and nutmeg and process until well combined, stopping the processor to scrape down the sides of the bowl with a spatula, if necessary. Add ⅔ cup oats and process until the oats are slightly chopped and the mixture sticks together (do not overprocess the mixture at this point or it will become extremely sticky and very difficult to work with). With a spatula, transfer the mixture to a small mixing bowl.

Place the remaining 2½ tablespoons oats on a large plate.

Divide the truffle mixture into 12 equal amounts (about 1 tablespoon each). Shape each into a ball. Gently roll the truffles, one at a time, in the oats, making sure the outside is coated. Serve immediately or store in an airtight plastic container for up to 3 days.

Makes 12 truffles

Per serving (2 truffles): 151 calories, 3 g protein, 34 g carbohydrates (4 g sugar), <1 g fat, 0 g saturated fat, 0 mg cholesterol, 3 g fiber, 3 mg sodium

Hollie Self, Season 4

Start your day with a moment for yourself. Whether it's reading a daily quote or enjoying your morning coffee, take a moment to establish your mind-set for the day ahead.

CINNAMON-SUGAR PRETZEL CANES

It's really fun to add edible glitter to cakes and desserts, especially at holiday time, to make them even more special and festive. And the nice thing about using glitter instead of sprinkles or other decorations is that they tend to be made from colored gelatin, not sugar, so they are virtually calorie free and, thus, consequence free.

---

2 tablespoons coconut sugar

½ teaspoon ground cinnamon

16 ounces whole wheat pizza dough (no more than 3 grams per 2-ounce serving), fresh or frozen and defrosted

2 tablespoons baking soda

Butter-flavored cooking spray

2 teaspoons egg substitute

Edible red glitter (optional)

Preheat the oven to 450°F. Line a large baking sheet with parchment paper. In a medium shallow bowl, mix the sugar and cinnamon. Set the mixture aside.

Fill a large soup pot one-third full with water. Bring the water to a boil.

Using a sharp knife or pastry cutter, cut the dough into 8 equal portions. Remove one of the portions to a cutting board. Roll the dough into a 24" rope that is an even thickness throughout. Cut the rope in half. Carefully secure the two halves at one end, then alternate folding each rope over the other until you reach the end, then secure the end by pressing it together. Shape the dough so that it resembles a candy cane. Set it aside. Repeat the process with the remaining dough, until you have 8 candy canes.

Add the baking soda to the boiling water. Mist a steamer insert with cooking spray, then place the candy canes in the insert so they lay flat in a single layer. (Work in batches, if necessary, carefully removing, then re-spraying the insert between each batch.) Place the steamer insert in the boiling water and cook for 1 to 2 minutes, or until they float. Using a slotted spoon to drain off any excess water, remove the canes to the prepared baking sheet in a single layer. Bake for 11 to 13 minutes, until they are lightly browned.

(continued)

Brush the top and sides of the pretzel canes lightly with egg substitute, making sure to coat the nooks and crannies. Immediately dip them into the cinnamon sugar mixture, pressing down slightly so they get well coated, then sprinkle remaining cinnamon sugar mixture over the pretzels so they are completely coated. Transfer them to a serving platter. Sprinkle them with glitter, if desired.

Makes 8 pretzels

Per pretzel: 142 calories, 4 g protein, 27 g carbohydrates (2 g sugar), 2 g fat, trace saturated fat, trace cholesterol, 3 g fiber, 192 mg sodium

Sam Poueu, Season 9

Know what you are eating. This is about your health, your life! Ask what ingredients are in the marinades for protein, for example. Some marinades have a lot of sugar, so be mindful of that.

RUBY-TOPPED LEAF CRISPS

I love to make these pretty "leaves" for my holiday entertaining tables. They look so festive and seasonal, and people are always impressed by them.

Be sure that you don't use low-carb tortillas to make these. Instead, look for a whole wheat brand that contains about 110 calories per serving and no more than a few grams of fiber; otherwise, they won't crisp properly.

---

1 reduced-fat whole wheat flour tortilla, not low-carb (7" diameter)

1 tablespoon egg substitute

½ teaspoon coconut sugar

¼ cup + 1 tablespoon all-natural low-fat ricotta cheese

2 teaspoons honey

¼ teaspoon freshly grated orange zest

3 tablespoons + 1 teaspoon pomegranate seeds (sometimes called pomegranate arils)

Preheat the oven to 400°F. Line a small baking sheet with parchment paper.

Place the tortilla on a cutting board or flat work surface and picture it as a clock before you begin cutting. Starting around 7 o'clock and ending around 5 o'clock, cutting 2" deep in half-circle fashion, create a "leaf" that is about 5½" to 6" long. Repeat 3 more times, going around the outsides of the tortilla, until you have 4 leaves. Then cut 1 more "leaf," making 2 half-circle slices, from the remaining piece of tortilla (you will have some small tortilla scraps leftover).

Lightly brush one side of the leaves with the egg substitute (you will have some egg left over), then sprinkle the sugar evenly among them. Transfer the leaves to the prepared baking sheet. Bake for 2 to 4 minutes per side, or until they are crisp throughout and lightly browned. Allow them to cool completely, for about 10 minutes.

Meanwhile, in a small bowl, stir together the ricotta, honey, and orange zest until well combined.

Flip the leaves over so the sugared side is facedown. Spread the ricotta mixture evenly among them (about 1 tablespoon on each), leaving the outer edges of the leaves bare. Transfer the leaves to a serving plate and sprinkle 2 teaspoons of pomegranate seeds over each. Serve immediately.

Makes 5 leaves

Per leaf: 55 calories, 3 g protein, 10 g carbohydrates (4 g sugar), 1 g fat, <1 g saturated fat, 5 mg cholesterol, <1 g fiber, 72 mg sodium

DECADENT DATE BARS

Though it will take a few extra minutes to chop the dates by hand, you'll end up with a better texture than you would if you pulsed them in a food processor. To create the perfect bars, you want the date pieces nicely chopped and bite-y, not at all paste-like.

If you like your bars gooey (like I do), it's best to cook them 2 or 3 minutes under what is recommended in the recipe. But if you prefer a more finished-looking, pretty bar, stick to the full cooking time.

Butter-flavored cooking spray

1 cup whole grain oat flour

½ teaspoon baking powder

¼ teaspoon salt

¾ cup egg substitute

¾ cup coconut sugar

1 teaspoon vanilla extract

1 pound pitted dates, chopped into small pieces

¼ cup finely shredded reduced-fat unsweetened coconut (I used Let's Do . . . Organic 40% less fat coconut)

¼ cup natural 70% cocoa mini dark chocolate chunks

Preheat the oven to 325°F. Lightly mist an 11" × 7" glass baking dish with cooking spray.

In a small mixing bowl, stir together the flour, baking powder, and salt. Set it aside.

In a medium mixing bowl, using a sturdy spatula, mix the egg substitute, sugar, and vanilla. Stir in the flour mixture until well combined, followed by the dates and 3 tablespoons of the chocolate chunks. Pour the mixture into the prepared dish. Sprinkle the coconut evenly over top, followed by the remaining 1 tablespoon chocolate.

Bake for 24 to 26 minutes, or until golden brown and a toothpick inserted in the center comes out sticky but not wet. Cool the bars on a wire rack until completely cool. Cut them into 16 bars, cleaning the knife in between each slice.

Makes 16 servings

Per serving: 170 calories, 3 g protein, 36 g carbohydrates (8 g sugar), 2 g fat, 1 g saturated fat, <1 mg cholesterol, 3 g fiber, 90 mg sodium

SWEETHEART STRAWBERRY TOWERS

This Naploean-inspired dessert is not only great for Valentine's Day, it's also an excellent way to show a little love any day of the year—because it's both delicious and heart-healthy.

It's best to chop the strawberries into small pieces to most evenly distribute them in this recipe. If you don't have a heart-shaped cookie cutter, you can use any shape cutter you have on hand.

Butter-flavored cooking spray

½ cup low-fat buttermilk

½ cup whole grain oat flour

1 large egg white, lightly beaten

1 tablespoon water

½ teaspoon baking soda

¼ teaspoon salt

¼ teaspoon vanilla extract

1 cup + 2 tablespoons "Cut the Crap" Whipped Topping (page 217)

1 cup + 2 tablespoons chopped strawberries

Lightly mist the inside of a 3¼"-wide and 2½"-tall metal (or heatproof) heart-shaped cookie cutter with cooking spray. (If you have more cutters, you can mist up to 4 cutters and make up to 4 cakes at once.)

In a small bowl, combine the buttermilk, flour, egg white, water, baking soda, salt, and vanilla. Whisk until just blended. Let stand for 10 minutes.

Heat a nonstick griddle or large nonstick skillet over medium heat until it is very warm. With an oven mitt, briefly remove the pan from the heat to mist it lightly with cooking spray. Return the pan to the heat. Immediately place the cookie cutter(s) in the pan (if using only one, place it close to one side, not in the center of the pan).

Pour 1 tablespoon of the batter in each cookie cutter and, using a butter knife, being careful not to scratch your pan, spread the batter into an even layer inside the cookie cutter(s). Let the batter set for 1 to 2 minutes, or until you can remove the cookie cutter without the batter running (run a butter knife lightly around the edges of the cutter if it doesn't remove easily). If you have only one cutter, as soon as you remove it, place it next to the first "heart cake" and pour another tablespoon of batter into it. Cook the first cake for 1 minute longer, or until bubbles appear on the top, then flip it and cook an additional 1 to 2 minutes, or until the bottoms are golden brown.

(continued)

Repeat in the same pan, wiping out the cookie cutter, if necessary, and re-spraying both the cutter and the pan until 12 heart cakes have been made. Transfer the finished cakes to a plate to cool slightly.

Place one heart cake on a serving plate. Top it with 1½ tablespoons of the whipped topping, followed by 1½ tablespoons of the strawberries. Repeat the layering process 2 more times, making 3 layers total (strawberries will be the final layer). Then repeat this on 3 more plates with the remaining cakes, whipped topping, and berries until you have 4 "towers." Serve immediately.

Makes 4 servings

Per tower: 99 calories, 4 g protein, 18 g carbohydrates (11 g sugar), 1 g fat, trace saturated fat, 2 mg cholesterol, 2 g fiber, 357 mg sodium

Migdalia Cancel, Season 9

When you're at a party and there's a dish made in a creamy sauce with chunks of chicken or beef, try to limit yourself to just the protein. Skip the bread and drink water before you start eating so you have a sense of fullness. If there are rich desserts, just limit yourself to a bite.

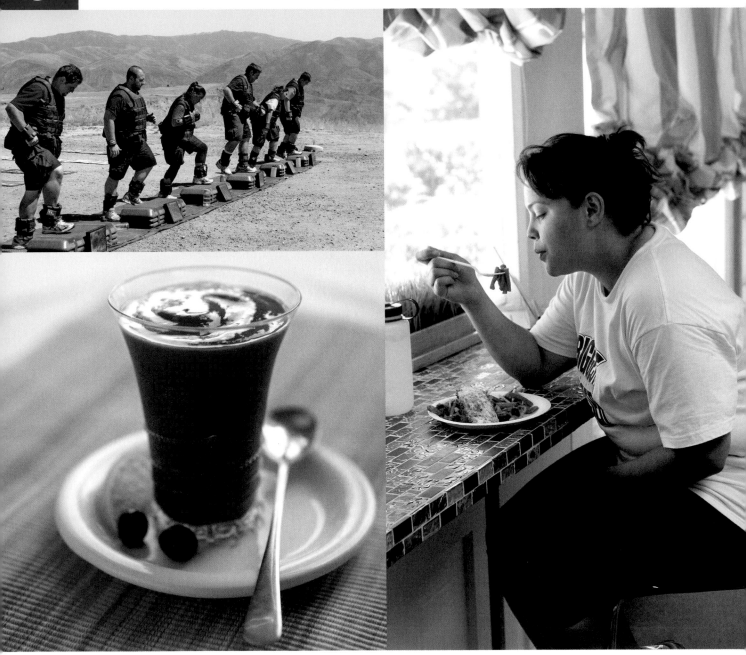

9

Sweet Sips

As the title suggests, all of the recipes in this chapter are sippable—and, as many *Biggest Losers* can attest, a lot of pleasure can be had from a few delicious sips rather than a 42-ounce guzzle.

The biggest source of liquid calories for a majority of the contestants when they arrive at the Ranch (and most other Americans) comes from drinking soda—and lots of it. Some contestants come to the Ranch drinking more calories a day in soda than they would soon be eating on their calorie budget! A lot of people drink soda when they want the taste of something sweet. The drinks in this chapter offer plenty of options to satisfy that sweet thirst without all of the sugar and calories contained in soda.

In many of these recipes, fruit plays a starring role, which makes sense, after all, since it's the high water content in many fruits that makes them so refreshing. In the Frozen Grape Champagne Flute (page 206), sweet frozen grapes take up the majority of the flute, which saves you at least 50 calories. And after you've finished your drink, you can savor the lovely, champagne-soaked grapes. Best of all, since you've barely had half a glass of champagne, you can feel free to enjoy another! Season 5 winner Ali Vincent says she still enjoys a good party and a nice cocktail, but now she's a lot less focused on the drinks and a lot more focused on dancing and catching up with friends. "It's not all about the food and the alcohol," she says. "It's about having real fun with friends."

Chef Devin Alexander says she usually adheres to a "drink *or* dessert" rule on most days and maybe a "drink *and* dessert" rule on special occasions. As long as you balance your sweets and your drinks, she points out, you won't leave a party or your own dinner table feeling uncomfortably stuffed.

In addition to alcohol, other high-calorie beverage pitfalls for many people are the rich, hot drinks we like to indulge in when the weather turns cool. Chef Devin's answer to hot chocolate with whipped cream and mocha lattes? Hot Vanilla (page 201), a creamy, satisfying treat that actually contains protein powder, making it the perfect postworkout treat.

Are you thirsty for more? Then keep reading . . .

SunShine Hampton, Season 9

Once I got home, there were definitely times when I felt like I was slipping back into my old routines, like staying up really late with my brothers. But I would be so tired in the morning that I knew I couldn't do that again. So if you do something that you know you shouldn't have, don't give up! Pick yourself up and keep going.

ICY CHAI SMOOTHIE

Chai lattes, ice blendeds, and other tea drinks have been popping up more and more in recent years. But most of them are full of sugar and calories, and when you're watching your weight, they're just not an option.

Well, there's no need to feel left out anymore! If you don't have The Biggest Loser *Vanilla Bean Protein Powder, you can substitute 150 calories' worth of a meal-replacement shake (one that has more carbs than protein per serving). If the powder you choose isn't sweet, you might also need a bit of added sweetener to create the blend as intended.*

1 cup unsweetened vanilla almond milk

¼ cup drained silken tofu

1 teaspoon vanilla extract

3 scoops *The Biggest Loser* Vanilla Bean Protein Powder, or 150 calories' worth of your favorite vanilla meal replacement shake

½ teaspoon chai spice blend

10 ice cubes

Add the almond milk, tofu, vanilla, protein powder, chai spice, and ice cubes to a blender with ice-crushing ability. Blend on high until the mixture is smooth and frothy. Divide evenly between 2 glasses. Serve immediately.

Makes 2 servings

Per serving: **116 calories, 11 g protein, 16 g carbohydrates (3 g sugar), 4 g fat, <1 g saturated fat, 0 mg cholesterol, 10 g fiber, 165 mg sodium**

Biggest Loser Trainer Tip: Bob Harper

It doesn't matter how far off track you've gone, if you just make a concerted effort every day—the smallest step—you can get control of your life again.

FROZEN BLUEBERRY MARGARITA

Though I've maintained a huge weight loss over the years, I confess that I still balk at giving up the occasional margarita. I know that most of the ones served at restaurants are full of sugar and calories, so I make my own lower-cal version at home. And because blueberries are the "star," you even get some fiber and antioxidant punch!

Before you start making the drinks, it's important to have all the ingredients ready. You don't want the blueberries and ice to melt while you're squeezing lemons and limes. If desired, you can rim your serving glass with lime juice and salt.

---

3 cups frozen blueberries

½ cup gold or silver tequila

½ cup freshly squeezed lemon juice

¼ cup freshly squeezed lime juice

¼ cup light agave nectar

24 ice cubes

4 lime wedges for garnish (optional)

Add the blueberries, tequila, lemon and lime juices, agave, and ice to a blender with ice-crushing ability. Blend on high until the mixture is smooth. Divide the margaritas among four 12-ounce glasses and serve immediately.

Makes 4 servings

Per serving: 188 calories, < 1 g protein, 33 g carbohydrates (27 g sugar), < 1 g fat, 0 g saturated fat, 0 mg cholesterol, 3 g fiber, < 1 g sodium

Sam Poueu, Season 9

I thought overindulging in alcohol might be a bigger problem for me after I got home from the Ranch because it was a big part of my life before. But once I saw friends who'd been drinking do stupid things, I realized that used to be me. Now I have the big picture in mind, and I put myself first.

HOT VANILLA

When I come home from a hard workout, I often crave a delicious protein shake or smoothie. But when the weather is cold, drinking a cold beverage just doesn't fit the bill. That's when this recipe provides the perfect solution. Sprinkling a little nutmeg or cinnamon on top makes this extra delicious. Move over, hot chocolate: It's time for a new cold-weather favorite!

---

8 ounces unsweetened vanilla almond milk

2 scoops *The Biggest Loser* Vanilla Bean Protein Powder, or 100 calories' worth of your favorite vanilla meal replacement shake

¼ teaspoon vanilla extract

Pinch ground nutmeg or ground cinnamon (optional)

Add the almond milk and protein powder to a small nonstick saucepan. Stir until the protein powder is completely dissolved, then stir in the vanilla. Place the pan over medium-low heat and heat the mixture, stirring frequently, until it is hot (it may look like the mixture is separating, but keep stirring and it will hold together). Pour the mixture into a 12-ounce mug. Top with nutmeg or cinnamon, if desired. Serve immediately.

Makes 1 serving

Per serving: **143 calories, 13 g protein, 20 g carbohydrates (4 g sugar), 5 g fat, 1 g saturated fat, 0 mg cholesterol, 13 g fiber, 280 mg sodium**

Michael Ventrella, Season 9 Winner

When I need to squeeze in a workout fast, I pull the treadmill in front of the TV and watch the news. Or if I have more time, I'll get lost in a movie. I'll bet I burn 800 calories that way!

HEART-HEALTHY SANGRIA

By now, we've all heard doctors or dietitians say that red wine is good for us. And it is—as long as we don't overdo it. This sangria is my answer to enjoying without overdoing. Since you combine fruit and soda with your red wine, it will feel a bit like you're consuming more red wine than you actually are. Note that you really can use your favorite inexpensive red wine for this since you add so much fruit and other flavors to it.

If you like having less of a punch of wine, or you want to extend the recipe to serve more people, or you want to conserve calories, feel free to add more soda. If you want to serve it by the pitcher instead of by the glass, just pour the whole can of soda into the pitcher and serve.

---

1 bottle (750 milliliters) red wine

½ large lemon, thinly sliced, visible seeds removed

1 lime, thinly sliced

1 firm pear (any variety), halved, cored, and cubed

1 medium orange

1 can (12 ounces) stevia-sweetened diet lemon-lime soda (I used Zevia Lemon-Lime Twist), chilled

Add the wine, lemon slices, lime slices, and pear cubes to a large (about 8-to-10 cup capacity) pitcher or serving bowl. Cut half of the orange into thin slices and add the slices to the wine mixture. Squeeze the juice from the remaining orange half into the wine mixture and stir well to combine. Cover the pitcher or bowl and refrigerate for 4 to 6 hours to allow the flavors to meld.

To serve, pour 1 cup of sangria (including fruit) into a serving glass. Top with 3 tablespoons of soda. Repeat with the remaining sangria and soda. Serve immediately or refrigerate (adding the soda just before serving) for up to 1 day.

Makes 6 (1-cup) servings

Per serving: **133 calories, trace protein, 14 g carbohydrates (5 g sugar), trace fat, 0 g saturated fat, 0 mg cholesterol, 2 g fiber, <1 mg sodium**

PEACH NO-BELLY BELLINI

This is a great recipe for using up those overripe peaches that are too soft for eating whole or slicing. Just make sure not to use white peaches for this recipe—they don't look nearly as pretty when pureed.

It's important for me to note that, like the other alcoholic beverages in the book, this isn't an every-day indulgence. But as part of The Biggest Loser *lifestyle, it's important not to deprive yourself. This is a great drink to make for special occasions and can be consumed in moderation as part of a balanced diet.*

---

2   small ripe peaches, peeled, pitted, and cut into chunks

1⅓   cups chilled prosecco or champagne, measured below the bubbles

Add the peaches to the bowl of a food processor fitted with a chopping blade. Process them until very smooth. Divide the mixture among four ¾-cup champagne flutes. Then divide the prosecco (or champagne) evenly among the champagne flutes, being careful as you pour not to let the prosecco overflow. Serve immediately.

Makes 4 servings

Per serving: 79 calories, <1 g protein, 7 g carbohydrates (5 g sugar), trace fat, trace saturated fat, 0 mg cholesterol, <1 g fiber, 0 mg sodium

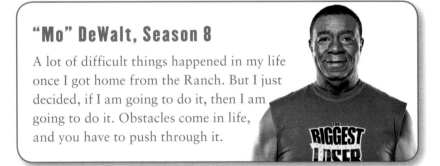

"Mo" DeWalt, Season 8

A lot of difficult things happened in my life once I got home from the Ranch. But I just decided, if I am going to do it, then I am going to do it. Obstacles come in life, and you have to push through it.

SKINNY SHIRLEY

Although the alcohol-free Shirley Temple is usually thought of as a kids' drink, this old-fashioned beverage also contains a ton of sugar, which doesn't exactly make it kid-friendly.

The word grenadine (the name of the syrup traditionally used to make Shirley Temples and other cocktails) comes from the French word grenade, which means "pomegranate." Grenadine is usually made from a combination of pomegranate juice and lots of sugar, so I've substituted pomegranate molasses here, which has no added sugar but tons of flavor. It can be purchased at many specialty food stores, natural food stores, and many liquor retailers.

1 teaspoon pomegranate molasses

1 can (12 ounces) stevia-sweetened diet lemon-lime soda (I used Zevia Lemon-Lime Twist), chilled

1 drop red food coloring

Ice cubes

1 fresh cherry or a few pomegranate arils (seeds)

Add the molasses to a 16-ounce narrow, tall glass. Stirring constantly, add just enough soda to dissolve the molasses. Add the remaining soda and food coloring. Stir well, just enough to combine. Add ice cubes, as desired, and garnish with the cherry or pomegranate. Serve immediately.

Makes 1 serving

Per serving: 18 calories, trace protein, 15 g carbohydrates (3 g sugar), trace fat, 0 g saturated fat, 0 mg cholesterol, trace fiber, 0 mg sodium

FROZEN GRAPE CHAMPAGNE FLUTE

Let's face it. Even those of us who are committed to being healthy want to have fun. The key to maintaining weight loss is creating ways to "participate" and not feel like you're sacrificing. This drink allows you to do just that.

Not only do the grapes come in handy to keep your drink cold, they also provide incentive to sip slowly and keep some champagne in your glass, since the grapes soak up the flavor of the champagne and become a fun treat themselves.

---

12 frozen seedless grapes (any variety)

⅓ cup chilled champagne or prosecco, measured below the bubbles

Add the grapes to a ¾-cup champagne flute. Top with champagne (or prosecco). Serve immediately. Use a cocktail stick to spear and eat the grapes once they are no longer frozen.

Makes 1 serving

Per serving: 94 calories, trace protein, 12 g carbohydrates (9 g sugar), trace fat, trace saturated fat, 0 mg cholesterol, <1 g fiber, 1 mg sodium

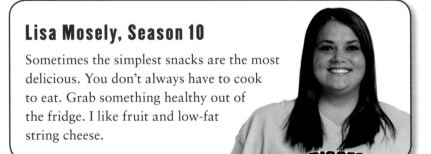

Lisa Mosely, Season 10

Sometimes the simplest snacks are the most delicious. You don't always have to cook to eat. Grab something healthy out of the fridge. I like fruit and low-fat string cheese.

MONKEY SHAKE

Over the years, I've seen many trainers make protein shakes simply by stirring together protein powder and milk or water—and I just don't get it. Even if I'm only going to have a shake made with milk and protein powder, I think it's so worth the effort to blend it with some ice cubes to create a frosty treat! Add in some cocoa powder and a banana, and it takes things to a whole new level.

1 cup unsweetened chocolate almond milk

3 scoops *The Biggest Loser* Chocolate Deluxe Protein Powder, or 150 calories' worth of your favorite chocolate meal replacement powder

1 tablespoon unsweetened cocoa powder

1 medium frozen banana, broken in half

10 ice cubes

Add the almond milk, protein powder, cocoa powder, banana halves, and ice cubes to a blender with ice-crushing ability. Blend on high until the mixture is smooth and frothy. Divide evenly between two 8-ounce serving glasses. Serve immediately.

Makes 2 servings

Per serving: 159 calories, 11 g protein, 29 g carbohydrates (12 g sugar), 4 g fat, <1 g saturated fat, 0 mg cholesterol, 12 g fiber, 173 mg sodium

Jerry Hayes, Season 7

Don't sell yourself short. The more you do, the stronger your heart and body will get. You'll be amazed.

MANGO LASSI MILKSHAKE

The mango lassi, a popular drink in parts of India (and served in many Indian restaurants in America), is usually made with yogurt, milk or water, mango, and sugar. Although there's no ice cream in this drink, it tastes a lot like a milkshake. It's thick, rich, and the perfect cure for a sudden sweet craving.

½ cup unsweetened vanilla almond milk

3 scoops *The Biggest Loser* Vanilla Bean Protein Powder, or your favorite vanilla-flavored meal replacement powder

1½ cups frozen mango chunks

¼ cup fat-free, fruit juice–sweetened vanilla yogurt (I used Cascade Fresh)

2 teaspoons freshly squeezed lime juice

10 ice cubes

Add the almond milk, protein supplement, mango, yogurt, lime juice, and ice cubes to a blender with ice-crushing ability. Blend on high until the mixture is smooth. Divide evenly between two 12-ounce glasses. Serve immediately.

Makes 2 servings

Per serving: 196 calories, 12 g protein, 42 g carbohydrates (27 g sugar), 2 g fat, <1 g saturated fat, 0 mg cholesterol, 12 g fiber, 135 mg sodium

CAN-DO CRANBERRY ORANGE SMOOTHIE

It's really worth using freshly squeezed orange juice in this smoothie, which provides a burst of citrus flavor that's hard to beat. You can use the fresh juice you find in cartons at the grocery store, too—just stay away from frozen concentrate.

Also, when buying frozen fruit, be sure to purchase brands that don't contain added sugars. The fruit is sweet enough on its own, and added sugar can cause blood sugar spikes and even cravings for some people.

¾ **cup frozen mango chunks**

½ **cup frozen cranberries**

¾ **cup freshly squeezed orange juice**

Add the mango, cranberries, and orange juice to a blender with ice-crushing ability. Blend on high until the mixture is smooth and frothy. Serve immediately.

Makes 1 serving

Per serving: 196 calories, 2 g protein, 49 g carbohydrates (39 g sugar), trace fat, trace saturated fat, 0 mg cholesterol, 6 g fiber, 3 mg sodium

Richard de Roque, Season 10

To lose weight, you need support, help, and knowledge. Ask for support and get the knowledge you need so the weight comes off and never comes back on.

10

Sinless Sauces, Dips, and Toppings

There's nothing like a drizzle or a dollop of a little something extra to make a dessert feel truly indulgent—but hot fudge, whipped cream, and cream cheese aren't exactly part of a healthy eating plan.

Chef Devin Alexander knows that the addition of these "extras" is exactly what makes a dessert feel truly special and decadent. That's why you'll find recipes such as "Cut the Crap" Whipped Topping (page 217)—a lower-calorie, all-natural alternative to the whipped toppings you'll find in a tub at the grocery store (many of which contain hydrogenated fats)—included in several of the recipes in this book. These indulgent-feeling toppings help make any healthy dessert taste (and look!) sinfully good.

But in addition to using these recipes to create the desserts in this book, these healthy makeovers of your favorite dessert "condiments" will soon become go-to staples in your home. Making ice cream sundaes with the kids? Why not whip up a batch of Chocolate Sauce (page 214) instead of using the stuff in a bottle made with high-fructose corn syrup? Want to add a dollop of something sweet to your healthy breakfast muffin? Throw together the Vanilla Cream Cheese Dip (page 219) and spread on a tablespoon.

The recipes that follow are so easy to make and so versatile that you'll continue to find new uses for them for years, as they become just another healthy staple you rely on to keep the pounds at bay without sacrificing the flavors you love.

CHOCOLATE SAUCE

I like to mix up a batch of this sauce and store it in a resealable plastic container in the refrigerator so I always have my own natural, homemade chocolate sauce on hand. It's so simple to whip together, and it lasts for weeks.

½ cup + 1 tablespoon agave nectar

¼ cup + 1 teaspoon unsweetened cocoa powder

Add the agave and cocoa powder to a medium resealable container (a round one will be easiest to mix in). Using a sturdy whisk, mix until well combined and no lumps remain from the cocoa powder.

Makes 12 (1-tablespoon) servings

Per serving: 47 calories, trace protein, 12 g carbohydrates (11 g sugar), trace fat, 0 g saturated fat, 0 mg cholesterol, trace fiber, 0 mg sodium

Elizabeth Ruiz, Season 10

To stay motivated, visualize all the fun things you'll be able to do once you lose the weight. I think about dancing all night, traveling, hiking, and parachuting out of a plane!

CHOCOLATE "FUDGE" SAUCE

I consider this recipe more necessary than almost any other in this book. Everyone who knows me knows that even though I've lost more than 55 pounds and maintained that loss for close to 20 years, I eat chocolate every day! This is my new favorite way to satisfy my chocolate cravings—an all-natural topper that contains only 45 calories per serving.

½ cup agave nectar

¼ cup + 1 tablespoon
unsweetened cocoa powder

Add the agave and cocoa powder to a medium resealable plastic container (a round one will be easiest to mix in). Using a sturdy whisk, mix until well combined and no lumps remain from the cocoa powder. Allow it to sit a few hours before using (it will taste fine immediately, but it thickens into a more fudgelike sauce over time).

Makes ¾ cup

Per serving (1 tablespoon): 45 calories, trace protein, 12 g carbohydrates (11 g sugar), trace fat, trace saturated fat, 0 mg cholesterol, <1 g fiber, trace sodium

RASPBERRY TAPENADE

All chocolate is made from the cacao (cocoa) bean. Cacao beans in their natural, unprocessed, unadulterated state are rich in nutrients and beneficial to health, which is why we sometimes hear that "chocolate is actually good for you." Cacao nibs have no added sugars and are raw and unprocessed. They are found at most natural food stores. If you cannot find them or would prefer not to invest in them, you can swap them out for dark chocolate pieces in this recipe. Just be sure to select a dark chocolate that is made from 70 percent or higher cacao.

1 cup raspberries	In a small resealable plastic container, mash the raspberries using a potato masher or fork until they break apart into small pieces and release their juices. Refrigerate for 30 minutes, or until chilled. Just before serving, stir in the cocoa nibs and stevia.

1 cup raspberries

½ tablespoon cacao nibs

8 drops liquid stevia, or to taste

In a small resealable plastic container, mash the raspberries using a potato masher or fork until they break apart into small pieces and release their juices. Refrigerate for 30 minutes, or until chilled. Just before serving, stir in the cocoa nibs and stevia.

Makes about ½ cup

Per serving (2 tablespoons): **17 calories, trace protein, 5 g carbohydrates (trace sugar), trace fat, trace saturated fat, 0 mg cholesterol, 2 g fiber, 4 mg sodium**

"CUT THE CRAP" WHIPPED TOPPING

Though you may be tempted to use a double boiler for this recipe, I would highly recommend using a saucepan and a large metal or heavy-duty glass mixing bowl that sits on top of the pan (and isn't too much larger than the pan). For maximum results, you need a large bowl so that a lot of air whips into the egg whites, creating volume. I've found that most double boiler inserts aren't quite big enough to allow that.

Please note that every time I've made this recipe, it yields a different amount of whipped topping, ranging from as few as 6 cups to as much as 8½ cups. Even slight variations in the size and temperature of the egg whites, the type of beaters you use, and the size of the bowl can make a difference. I've calculated the nutritional information based on 6 cups. Store any excess whipped topping in the freezer for up to a couple of weeks.

¾ cup light agave nectar

3 large egg whites, at room temperature

½ teaspoon cream of tartar

Add water to a medium saucepan until it is about one-quarter full. Bring the water to a boil over high heat.

Off the heat, combine the agave, egg whites, and cream of tartar in a large metal or heavy-duty glass mixing bowl (one that will fit onto the top of your saucepan). Beat on medium-high with an electric mixer fitted with beaters until well blended.

Place the bowl over the pot of boiling water. (For safety, be sure to wear an oven mitt while holding the bowl over the heat, as it will get very hot.) Beat for 7 minutes, or until stiff peaks form, occasionally running the beaters around the sides of the bowl to scrape any of the mixture. Remove the bowl from the water and continue beating, rotating the bowl and scraping down the sides with the beaters as you do, for 5 to 7 minutes longer, or until the mixture is thick, very fluffy, and has very stiff peaks.

Makes about 6 cups

Per serving (1 tablespoon): **8 calories, trace protein, 2 g carbohydrates (2 g sugar), 0 g fat, 0 g saturated fat, 0 mg cholesterol, 0 g fiber, 2 mg sodium**

YOGURT CHEESE

Yogurt cheese is easy to make and so worth the extra effort. It's much less processed than any fat-free cream cheese I've encountered. When made with fat-free yogurt, yogurt cheese has 6 grams of fat per 2-tablespoon serving less than light cream cheese, but tastes very similar in many applications, including the Mini Key Lime Cheesecake Pies (page 139).

1 **container (64 ounces) fat-free, all natural plain yogurt**

You'll need 2 clean, lint-free dish towels, a large bowl, and 12" or longer metal skewers, plastic chopsticks, or other clean, sturdy sticks.

Lay one dish towel flat on a clean work surface next to the sink. Spoon half of the yogurt (about 4 cups) into the center of the towel. Carefully pull the towel up, connecting it in the center just over the yogurt, creating a ball of yogurt in the bottom of the towel. Gently twist the towel one or two times, or until a steady stream of liquid starts to drip (do not twist so much that the yogurt squishes out of the towel).

Once there is no longer a steady stream (it's okay if it's just dripping), carefully secure the pouch with a sturdy rubber band or twine, making sure the rubber band is as close to the yogurt as possible. Thread the skewers underneath the rubber band on opposite sides of the yogurt pouch. Place the skewers over a large bowl, making sure that the yogurt pouch is suspended and not touching the bottom of the bowl.

Repeat the process with the remaining yogurt and towel. Refrigerate overnight. Discard the liquid in the bottom of the bowl, then unwrap the yogurt cheese and transfer it to a resealable plastic container. Refrigerate it for up to 3 days.

Makes 4 cups

Per cup: 220 calories, 26 g protein, 32 g carbohydrates (26 g sugar), 0 g fat, 0 g saturated fat, 10 mg cholesterol, 0 g fiber, 300 mg sodium

VANILLA CREAM CHEESE DIP

You can make a batch of this scrumptious dip and keep it in your refrigerator to have on hand for several days. I use it in my Berry Skewers 'n Dip (page 85), Blueberry Cream Cheese "Strudel" (page 143), and A-List Apple Danishes (page 159), but feel free to get creative and enjoy it in new ways, too. It's the perfect accompaniment to a fresh fruit plate.

½ cup reduced-fat cream cheese (sometimes called Neufchatel cheese)

½ teaspoon vanilla extract

1 tablespoon + 1 teaspoon light agave nectar

Add the cream cheese, vanilla, and agave to a small mixing bowl. Using an electric mixer fitted with beaters, beat on high speed until smooth. Serve immediately.

Makes 8 (1-tablespoon) servings

Per serving: 45 calories, 1 g protein, 4 g carbohydrates (3 g sugar), 3 g fat, 2 g saturated fat, 10 mg cholesterol, 0 g fiber, 70 mg sodium

Acknowledgments

Devin Alexander

"Over the moon" doesn't begin to describe how excited I am to be expanding *The Biggest Loser* cookbook series and to continue to be a part of *The Biggest Loser* family. And it's all because of so many ridiculously awesome people whom I can always count on:

Thanks to the whole team at Rodale, particularly Julie Will, who happens to be a brilliant editor *and* who knows the value (and necessity!) of guilty pleasures like chocolate with peanut butter and a bit of alcohol. To project editor superhero Nancy N. Bailey, who makes sure the trains run on time. To designer Christina Gaugler, who made the pages look so enticing with the help of killer photographers Mitch Mandel and Tom MacDonald. To the oh-so-talented and sweet Melissa Roberson, who spent hours writing the nonrecipe portions of this book. To publisher Karen Rinaldi and publicity goddesses Emily Weber and Yelena Nesbit. And to Robin Shallow, who has supported me for years and might possibly be the "Real-Life Wonder Woman." Really. I mean it. I think she is!

To Dr. Michael Dansinger, for keeping my and Julie's chocolate-and-peanut butter loves in check while still giving us freedom to create.

To the ultimate coordinator Edwin Karapetian. And to Reveille's Vice President of Brand Development and Production Chad Bennett, who's worked with me on every book and whom I absolutely adore beyond words.

To the producers and executives of *The Biggest Loser*, particularly Mark Koops, Todd Nelson, and J. D. Roth of 3 Ball Productions, who made me the happiest girl ever when they first invited me into *The Biggest Loser* family. To Kim Niemi, Neysa Siefert, and Joni Camacho from NBC Universal and to Dave Broome and Yong Yam from 25/7 Productions, who simply rock!

To Bob Harper and Jillian Michaels, for embracing me and my work. To all *Biggest Loser* contestants who've spent time in my kitchen and let me spend time in theirs, inspiring so many of my creations. To Chef Cameron and Renee Jarvis of *The Biggest Loser* Resort, who are amazing!

To Katie and the team at Farmer's Market Organic Pumpkin, who supplied us with desperately needed canned pumpkin.

To my test kitchen goddess, Stephanie Farrell, and go-to gal, Angela Nehmens, who have truly become so integral in my kitchen and my life that I think of them as sisters as well as coworkers. And to recipe testers Erin Preuss, Vanessa Werkheiser, and Ryoko Yoshida, who managed to keep the recipes in check while adding tons of fun through the constant (fruit) sugar highs we all experienced! And to Jessica Bright, who lent a number of ideas.

A very special thanks to publicist Ashley Sandberg, Carrie Simons, and Jim Eber, whose advice and guidance is irreplaceable! And "Rock Star" James Emley, who rescued me from gaining weight and going insane with his "let's go" spirit that got me outdoors and kept a smile on my face even when the cakes still didn't want to cooperate at 2 a.m.!

Melissa Roberson

My deepest thanks must always go to every single *Biggest Loser* contestant past and present. You share your stories and dreams, fears and hopes with me. I am always moved by what you have to say and feel privileged to listen. You are what make my work meaningful and special.

Thank you to Devin Alexander for always being cheerful and available and full of energy. I will always be impressed by what you have accomplished. To my other *Biggest Loser* family, including Cheryl Forberg, RD, and Chad Bennett, thanks for the emails and phone calls that keep me on track—emotionally and professionally! Bob Harper, it's always fun to chat with you and get a little Southern repartee going.

To my book editor, Julie Will, I think we have a mind meld at this point. Always, always a pleasure to work with you.

And grateful thanks to my long-suffering husband, Sal, and kitty cats, Chet and Kitty Carlisle. We are family!

Index

Underscored page references indicate sidebars and tables. **Boldface** references indicate photographs.

Also available in the *New York Times* best-selling Biggest Loser series...

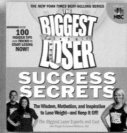